EUROPEAN CASES IN ENTREPRENEURSHIP

EUROPEAN CASES IN ENTREPRENEURSHIP

Edited By
THOMAS M. COONEY & RICKIE A. MOORE

BLACKHALL
Publishing

Paperback ISBN: 978-1-84218-144-7
Hardback ISBN: 978-1-84218-147-8

This book was typeset by Paragon Prepress, Inc. for
Blackhall Publishing
33 Carysfort Avenue
Blackrock
Co. Dublin
Ireland.
e-mail: info@blackhallpublishing.com
www.blackhallpublishing.com

Printed in the UK by Athenaeum Press

Table of Contents

Foreword

In many ways it is quite fitting that the Faculty of Business at the Dublin Institute of Technology is so strongly associated with this book. In addition to being members of ECSB (European Council for Small Business) and EFMD (European Foundation for Management Development), one of our colleagues is to be the next president of ECSB. Furthermore, we have had the privilege of sponsoring each of the ECSB Case Study competitions since its inception in 2004. But it is the Faculty's long history in the use of case studies in its pedagogy that makes our sponsorship of this book most appropriate.

The Faculty introduced the use of case studies into its teaching in the late 1970s, and for over thirty years now case studies have been used as the primary method of teaching throughout the final year of our degree programmes. Case studies are additionally employed to support teaching in the earlier years of all programmes in order to enhance the understanding by the student of the application of theory to practice. A number of our staff are well recognised as case study writers in their own areas of business expertise and have contributed significantly to the development of this form of teaching both nationally and internationally. Indeed, the world final of the marketing case study competition for undergraduate students was hosted by the Faculty in May 2007.

But the relationship between this book and the Faculty of Business is not just located within the use of case studies. The Project Development Centre was established in 1983 to encourage and stimulate the development of indigenous enterprise by offering an innovative programme to graduates who wanted to start their own business and has since expanded its range of programmes to cater for a broader range of target audiences. The Bolton Trust was established in 1986 by staff of DIT and continues to provide incubation space and related services to a wide array of small companies.

Modules in entrepreneurship were added to undergraduate courses in the early 1990s and in more recent times the Faculty developed an MSc in Business and Entrepreneurship, in addition to a dedicated stream in entrepreneurship on its MBA programme. The Faculty also provides modules in entrepreneurship at undergraduate and postgraduate levels to the Faculties of Science, Engineering, Art, and Food and Tourism.

I would like to encourage all readers of this book to use case studies as part of their teaching programme. It has been our experience that students have benefited significantly from the inclusion of case studies in the pedagogy and employers have noted how quickly the students have been able to contribute positively within their career positions. We at the Faculty of Business are happy to share our learning and experience with any individual or institution that wishes to develop this form of learning. I invite you to contact us with any questions that you might wish to ask. I shall conclude by congratulating Tom and Rickie on their initiative and wish them every success with the book.

Best regards

Paul O'Sullivan
Director
Faculty of Business
Dublin Institute of Technology

The Dublin Institute of Technology provides full-time and part-time programmes to over 22,000 students across the whole spectrum of higher education. DIT undertakes this work in an innovative, responsive, caring and flexible learning environment, with state-of-the-art facilities and the most advanced technology available. It is committed to providing access to higher education for students of different ages and backgrounds, and to achieving quality and excellence in all aspects of its work. This commitment extends to the provision of teaching, research, development and consultancy services for industry and society, with due regard to the technological, commercial, social and cultural needs of the community that it serves.

The Dublin Institute of Technology offers a wide range of 'Executive Education' programmes through online learning, classroom lectures and on-site workshops. The Faculty of Business is the largest business school in Ireland and it provides a range of entrepreneurship modules across the Faculties of Business, Science, Art, Engineering, and Food and Tourism. The Faculty of Business also offers a one-year MSc in Business and Entrepreneurship which is dedicated to transforming science, engineering, social science, business and technology graduates into leaders who will guide and create tomorrow's businesses. In doing so it addresses Ireland's need to remain competitive by cultivating cross-functional, entrepreneurial graduates. The MBA programme also offers a dedicated stream in Entrepreneurship.

DIT additionally provides a number of entrepreneurship support organisations targeting a variety of audiences. The "Institute for Minority Entrepreneurship" was established to offer the different minority groups in Ireland equal opportunity through entrepreneurship education and training. The following groups are considered by the Institute to be "minority entrepreneurship groups": ethnic, grey, disabled, travellers, gay, female, Irish-speaking, prisoners and socio-economically disadvantaged. The primary objective of the Institute is to bring significant benefit to its target audiences by researching the needs of these minority entrepreneurship groups, developing appropriate training programmes and materials, and delivering these programmes in the most effective manner possible for each individual group.

The Project Development Centre (PDC) was initiated by the Dublin Institute of Technology in 1983, and operates under the Directorate of External Affairs. It has been instrumental in encouraging and stimulating the development of indigenous enterprise through a range of activities. Today the PDC is one of the leading centres for enterprise and innovation. It provides a comprehensive range of services and products, including skills development programmes, incubation space and facilities, business counselling, funding, and access to research and development expertise. Meanwhile, the Bolton Trust was established in 1986 by staff of DIT, and the Trust currently has over 200 members. It is a voluntary organisation, actively committed to assisting people create sustainable business. The Bolton Trust's centrepiece is the Docklands Innovation Park, which encourages and promotes new business enterprise through a range of facilities dedicated to early stage entrepreneurs.

The Faculty of Business at DIT has a strong history of working at European level through its active participation in a large number of EU programmes and its dynamic membership of organisations such as EFMD (European Foundation for Management Development) and ECSB (European Council for Small Business). As recently as 2001, it hosted the EFMD/EISB Conference, which attracted delegates from twenty-two countries and offered a programme that was very well received. The Faculty of Business would welcome the opportunity to renew partnerships with old friends and to begin new relationships with institutions with which it has not yet established collaboration. Further details of what it offers to its partners can be found at <http://www.dit.ie>.

EM LYON, one of the oldest business schools in the world, is a European institution in the French "Grande Ecole" tradition. Founded in 1872, EM LYON is devoted to lifelong learning through entrepreneurial and international management. EM LYON believes that:

- Its entrepreneurial and educational mission assists in stimulating the social responsibility of its participants, thus giving them all the support needed to achieve business success in the various cultural and economic systems around the world.
- Its know-how in training is based both on theory and on day-to-day company management.
- Its distinctive expertise is founded on teaching innovation and an entrepreneurial approach to management education.

Within the EM LYON Entrepreneurship Centre is an incubator that is dedicated to helping students and entrepreneurs pursue their entrepreneurial ventures. For the last twenty-five years, EM LYON has coached and mentored hundreds of entrepreneurs, and has helped launch over 550 companies that created 10,000 jobs, including a number of student-owned ventures. As part of its range of activities, the Entrepreneurship Centre has a number of programmes that provide training, support, advice and assistance for entrepreneurs who will either create or acquire a venture, and that foster the entrepreneurial spirit among engineers and science-based students in biotechnologies, high tech, services, etc. EM LYON's students regularly win prizes at various national, European and international business plan competitions.

The "Entrepreneurial Spirit", the credo of EM LYON, is omnipresent and has influenced and permeated the curricula of all the programmes (graduate, open, Executive Education, etc.) and research at EM LYON. With entrepreneurship, the international perspective is one of the major teaching specialisations of EM LYON. A melting pot with some sixty nationalities, the campuses at EM LYON are all extensively multicultural. As part of its collaboration with its partners around the world EM LYON opened branch campuses in Geneva (Switzerland) and Shanghai (China) in September 2007. Annually, EM LYON trains almost 3,000 students, and 5,000 managers enrol in its Executive Education programmes. EM LYON offers a European Master in Management (triple degree, triple campus, triple alumni network, triple educational approach) with its partners from Aston (UK) and Munich (Germany), an MSc in Management, a Masters in European Business, a PhD in Management programme, twelve specialised masters, an International and an Executive MBA, a special diploma programme for CEOs and senior managers of SMEs, a Certificate Programme in General Management, an Advanced Management Programme for Chinese executives, and a number of custom-built Concentration Programmes for partner schools and firms from around the world that would either like to have an international study programme in France or in Europe, or have EM LYON train its employees locally, in their countries.

Being among the best European business schools[1] requires the development of academic knowledge at an international level but also of expertise driven by business realities. The mission of the core faculty of EM LYON is to provide all students and participants in its programmes with high-quality training. The 110-strong faculty is supported by several content experts, business executives, professionals, consultants and professors from universities, business schools firms and organisations around the world. For more than twenty years, EM LYON has strongly invested in new educational methods and technologies. Today, it boasts highly innovative, award-winning experiential learning systems designed for both graduate and executive programmes. This new form of teaching combines the search for efficiency in the learning process with participant motivation.

EM LYON has a long-standing tradition in academic and applied research. EM LYON faculties are actively involved in multiple research projects and several national, European and international academic and professional networks, and play a prominent role in some top tier journals and academic associations. EM LYON works closely with partner companies in research programmes to identify and find solutions to emerging management problems in fields such as entrepreneurship, innovation and management of strategic change. EM LYON is one of the few select institutions worldwide to have received the "triple crown" accreditation by the three leading international accreditation bodies – AACSB,[2] EQUIS[3] and AMBA[4] (international systems of quality accreditation). More information can be had by visiting its website at: <http://www.em-lyon.com>

NOTES

[1] *Financial Times* ranking, December 2006: EM LYON ranked 13th among the top 55 business schools.

[2] Association to Advance Collegiate Schools of Business International.

[3] European Quality Improvement System.

[4] Association of MBAs.

The European Council for Small Business (ECSB) is a not-for-profit organisation whose main objective is to advance the understanding of entrepreneurship and to improve the competitiveness of SMEs (small to medium-sized enterprises) in Europe. ECSB facilitates the creation and distribution of new knowledge through research, education and the open exchange of ideas between professions and across national and cultural borders. ECSB also cooperates with various EU and governmental institutions interested in improving the understanding and development of small businesses and entrepreneurship in general. The network of ECSB's members covers nearly the whole of Europe geographically, with over 500 members from across thirty countries. Through its affiliation to the International Council for Small Business, the European network is also connected to the global academic and professional small business community.

ECSB organises high-quality conferences for its members, such as the RENT conference in cooperation with EIASM (the European Institute for Advanced Studies in Management), in order to facilitate and enhance the exchange of knowledge within the ECSB membership. The exchange and creation of knowledge is also possible through the Internet platform that it enables on its website (<http://www.ecsb.org>). ECSB offers many additional benefits to its members including:

- Four issues annually of the *Journal of Small Business Management.*
- The *ICSB Bulletin,* which carries information about member activities, interest group issues, conference programmes and organisational developments from around the world.
- The *ECSB Newsletter,* which contains information regarding research, education and other activities in Europe.

- Access to international conferences at reduced registration fees (e.g. the ICSB World Conference, the RENT Conference, etc).
- Other small business journals (e.g. the *International Small Business Journal*) at reduced rates.
- Participation in the European Doctoral Programme on Entrepreneurship and Small Business Management.

You can join the ECSB network by filling in the membership application on the website or by sending an e-mail to the ECSB secretariat (info@ecsb.org). After the receipt of the membership fee you will receive a password for the membership database on the website and you will be entitled to the full membership benefits.

The European Foundation for Management Development (EFMD) is an international membership organisation, based in Brussels, Belgium. With more than 650 member organisations from academia, business, public service and consultancy in seventy-five countries, EFMD provides a unique forum for information, research, networking and debate on innovation and best practice in management development.

EFMD is recognised globally as an accreditation body of quality in management education and has established accreditation services for business schools and business school programmes, corporate universities and technology-enhanced learning programmes. Additionally, EFMD:

- Has over 30 years of experience in the coordination of projects and activities that fosters an active dialogue and exchange between companies and academic organisations.
- Contributes to a search for, and generation of, new ideas for a continual enhancement of management thinking and practices.
- Maintains a series of on-going activities enabling its members to learn, share and network, which helps contribute to a better understanding of the continual changes in the business and management education environments.
- Initiates short events on highly topical issues bringing business executives and distinguished academics together.
- Provides a context and environment that leads to professional networking and bridges the divide between the academic and business worlds.
- Runs the European Quality Improvement System (EQUIS), which is the leading international system of quality assessment, improvement and accreditation of higher education institutions in

management and business administration. 110 schools have so far been accredited from across thirty-two different countries.

- Manages international projects in Asia, the Commonwealth of Independent States (CIS) and the Arab world and has strong relationships with sister associations in Eastern Europe, Central Asia, Central America, the United States, Canada and Australasia.
- Provides the platform for exposure to new learning environments. We generate and disseminate knowledge throughout the network for the benefit of our members. This ability to share allows for a better understanding of the latest developments in management development.

EFMD advances excellence in management development in Europe and worldwide by building links between leading business schools and companies, creating and disseminating knowledge on best practices and changing trends and providing access to benchmarking tools and accreditations (EQUIS, EPAS, CEL, CLIP). Visit <http://www.efmd.org>.

Introduction

Entrepreneurship as a concept, a discipline and a practice is unarguably global. Few cultures, if any, are resisting the rollercoaster push to develop entrepreneurs. Inspired by the tremendous impact that entrepreneurship has had economically in the USA since the 1970s and 1980s, nations around the world are seeking to create their own success stories by embarking on their own entrepreneurial revolution. While some nations consider this entrepreneurial revolution as a "no choice" situation for solving a number of national (and eventually global) economic problems, the journey is not necessarily as simple and as straightforward as it may sound, or as some believe it to be.

The diversity with which Europe has been built offers an extremely rich variety of entrepreneurial contexts, situations and cultures. In conceiving *European Cases in Entrepreneurship* our ambition was not only to depict this diversity, but to also provide a comprehensive and articulated source of insightful pan-European entrepreneurship cases that can be used in entrepreneurship education. Moving from the reflection idea stage in a local setting to that of global entrepreneurship, and spanning the sectors of services, high technology, innovative products and social entrepreneurship, this volume provides a series of thought-provoking cases designed to illustrate the challenges of the entrepreneurial journey.

In assembling a number of entrepreneurial examples, this book presents a variety of entrepreneurs and their interesting stories, as well as the problems and issues that they face in their ventures. Our intention is to facilitate a greater understanding of entrepreneurial skills, knowledge and frameworks that people develop while pursuing entrepreneurial opportunities. In undertaking the cases, students will explore and review several dimensions of different theories, processes and practices that are integral to the study of entrepreneurship.

It has been increasingly widely recognised in recent years that there is an urgent need to develop European cases in entrepreneurship that can be used with students to show them what is possible in terms of entrepreneurial opportunity across Europe. However, this book is only a starting point in the long-term goal of arming teachers of entrepreneurship with the appropriate material required to light the imagination of our students of entrepreneurship. As Alexander Pope once wrote, "young minds are not vessels to be filled, but fires to be ignited".

Best regards,

Thomas M. Cooney and Rickie A. Moore

Case Abstracts

FRENCH ART OF LIVING (ALAIN FAYOLLE)

The main pedagogical aim of the case is to lead the learner to take a position regarding the decision of whether or not to commit oneself to the creation of a new business. In the case, the process has started and the project is in a sufficiently advanced stage of development for the prospective entrepreneurs to find themselves confronted with the difficulty of taking the classic decision that can be summarised by, "should I stay or should I go?" Do I continue with the project and commit myself even more or do I stop everything and concentrate on looking for a regular job? The situation analysed is typical of numerous business creation projects imagined and/or developed by students, higher education graduates and executives who find themselves facing alternative career paths. The dilemma between the appeal and relative attractiveness of these different professional (and personal) scenarios, as well as the resistance to change, usually conditions the option that will finally be taken. Nevertheless, there are ways of influencing some key factors (reduction to the resistance and improvement in the attraction of the creation project) of which potential entrepreneurs and the professionals that support them should be aware.

IVIEWCAMERAS (DAVID MOLIAN)

In September 2002 Peter (Pete) Rankin is leaving his MBA programme to launch a new Internet-based venture, IViewCameras. The price of wireless CCTV (closed-circuit television) has fallen dramatically, creating a new marketing opportunity. To launch his venture, Pete has reached agreement with an established Internet-based retailer, InternetCamerasDirect, to incubate IViewCameras in return for shares. InternetCamerasDirect can provide IViewCameras with an existing infrastructure for sales, procurement and fulfilment. However, Pete's presentation of his venture to external reviewers has gone badly. A venture capitalist doubts whether a business model that proposes both to sell manufacturers' brands and build an IViewCameras brand is viable, and questions whether the business is truly sustainable without an intellectual property base. Pete is left to ponder whether the concept is fatally flawed, or whether he should fall back on his self-belief and instinct that this is the right product at the right time. IViewCameras is a study in the second wave of Internet-based ventures that followed the dot.com shakeout of 2000, and the different approach adopted by one such entrepreneur.

NovoGEL (THIERRY VOLERY AND MARTINA JAKL)

Transforming starches into synthetic products has been a dream cherished by industry and science for a long time. All solutions up to now have had one serious drawback: the products have not been waterproof. However, two Zurich-based entrepreneurs, Rolf Müller and Federico Innerebner, made a breakthrough in 2001. With a special method they were able to produce made-to-measure gels out of starch. This method is not only used to produce plastics that are impervious to water, it is also a platform technology, the potential applications of which extend from foodstuffs to medical technology. From the beginning, it was clear to Rolf Müller and Federico Innerebner that this could be the basis of their own business. A series of decisions had to be made in order to exploit the opportunity: which markets should be approached, and in what order? What should the organisational structure best suited for this look like? This case focuses on the evaluation of opportunities when the entrepreneur has developed a platform technology (a technology with several applications). The immediate issue is to decide what application should be developed and what the appropriate market is. Other basic issues that need to be addressed include market research and the choice of a suitable form of organisation to exploit the technology.

BEYOND PRODUCTS (SOPHIE MANIGART)

Peter Van Riet, a young entrepreneur and enthusiastic snowboarder, has developed a revolutionary snowboard binding for which he holds patent rights in Europe and the USA. A first prototype has already been successfully tested. His business and marketing plan show that there is room for a new binding, introduced into the fragmented snowboard binding market by a small and young company. He targets the European and North American markets in the first place, expanding to a global brand as the company takes off. He will mainly sell through smaller national distributors. His goal is to develop the company over time into a fully-fledged snowboard branch, not only offering bindings but also clothing and accessories. Having invested all of his time and savings of approximately €350,000 in product development, patent rights and initial marketing expenses, he is currently looking for a €300,000 cash investment by a syndicate of four business angels who he has found through a local business angel network. This money is needed for further product development, prototyping and testing, and for marketing and sales. The key issues that he cannot resolve is what equity percentage would be fair to the business angels, without diluting the founders' position too much, and also compensating them honestly for their efforts until now? In order to answer this question, he has developed a full financial plan with profit and loss (P&L) and cash flow statements. He moreover has gathered information on the relative valuation of quoted companies in the sports apparel business.

BOBLBEE (BENOÎT LELEUX AND JOACHIM SCHWASS)

The case summarises the personal situation for one of the founders, Patrik Bernstein, and the choices he made in order to pursue his dream of becoming an entrepreneur. It describes the opportunity (the backpack Boblbee), its technical details, the marketing and supply chain, and the market in which it is supposed to compete. Overall the case gives the students the opportunity to:

- Evaluate Boblbee as an entrepreneurial opportunity.
- Consider a potential investment opportunity.
- Evaluate the major risk factors and challenges going forward and how to manage them.
- Define Boblbee's Customer Value Proposition.
- Develop a comprehensive internally consistent business model, covering supply chain and production, marketing and sales, entry and growth strategies, financing, etc.

NEWS AGGREGATOR ONLINE (CHRISTIAN SERAROLS AND JOSÉ MARÍA VECIANA)

"News Aggregator Online S.L. (NAO)" describes the process of venture creation and evolution of a high technological venture spin-off from a university by a group of young industrial engineers. It highlights the different stages that the entrepreneurial team went through, from the idea to the edge of the growth stage, and the critical junctures that they had to face in each phase. Overall, the case focuses on the difficulties between the different members of the entrepreneurial team and how they managed them. The case also opens a window into the identification of a new stage (redefinition) that hardly exists in the literature. This redefinition stage seems to be critical in the process of creation and growth of the company. The case is organised as it follows: Section 1 introduces the background to the case; Section 2 describes the technology, products and services developed by NAO; Section 3 focuses on the background of the founding team; Section 4 discusses the different stages of the process of venture creation (origin, planning and implementation); a brief note on the working team, product development and first redefinition stage can be found in Section 5; Section 6 focuses on the problems in getting finance; and finally Section 7 highlights the most important discussions among the founding team regarding the future business concept and growth strategy of NAO.

ACADEMIC WORK (KENT THORÉN)

Finding an opportunity and defining a business idea is only the starting point of entrepreneurship. Following this is a long succession of many, and sometimes much greater, challenges. Not only is it difficult to make the firm succeed, success tends to, in itself, bring about new problems. At Academic Work, a Swedish agency specialising in providing companies with temporary help from students, growth has been tremendous. However, under the surface, there is a constant struggle for achieving focused and effective activities, in order to keep maintaining both top- and bottom-line business growth. At the same time, managers have also become increasingly aware of a number of issues caused by the associated organisational growth (i.e. the increasing number of permanent employees and organisational units). In short, growth management turned out to be much more multifaceted than the entrepreneurs first thought. This case study follows Academic Work during its initial growth phase and presents a few of the managerial challenges that occurred. Some of these concern traditional organisational issues, such as the division of labour and finding an appropriate span of control for managers. Other issues are more advanced, for instance whether, how and when more systematic control systems should be used. Finally, it turns out that while the firm has matured, the industry has been maturing alongside it. In other words, the strategic situation changed, leaving managers with some tough decisions regarding the future directions of the business. In summary, the case presents a number of issues relevant to anybody who is interested in strategy, organisation and control of fast-growing single-business firms.

H&H Oy (Jane Silver)

The Pessa family had owned forests in the northern region of Tampere for generations. They had tended the forest, felling trees for the local pulp and paper factories, as well as providing wood for furniture. Originally, before the large pulp and papermaking factories were built, the Pessa family (like many local foresters) had their own pulp-making capabilities. Timo Pessa, Harri and Hanna's father, had developed the family business into a thriving tourist activity holiday centre. One of the activities was built on the existing pulp-making capabilities and was entitled "From Wood to Paper". Harri and Hanna had developed the handcrafted paper activity into a craft business. The business expanded rapidly and in order to meet demand moved to the Finlayson complex in Tampere. Orders for handcrafted papers continued to rise, including export orders for Norway and Sweden. The twins are at a crossroads with the business. There were three elements to their business: the farmhouse activity holidays, which are self-sustaining; the forestry business, which is giving cause for concern in light of the changing global industry; and the handcrafted paper business, which is expanding. Looking at their portfolio of businesses they concluded that the only way forward was to expand the handcrafted paper business into Europe. The problem they faced was they had no knowledge about doing business in different cultures. They decided to employ a student to investigate the pitfalls of doing business in Europe and suggested that as a starting point the student look at an online guide: <http:www.businessculture.org>

South Hill Enterprise (Thomas M. Cooney)

This case is about a not-for-profit organisation in which each member of staff (excluding the supervisors) has some form of intellectual disability. The goals of the organisation are to provide a safe, happy work environment for people with intellectual disabilities, to create greater awareness of the abilities of people with intellectual disabilities, to create and maintain close links with local communities, to generate income for the development of the enterprise and to provide quality handmade produce for its customers. The business has three principal groups of products: chocolate, bakery and preserves (jams). The most profitable of these, and most exciting in terms of market potential, are the chocolate products. However, South

Hill Enterprise does not wish to secure too many large orders because the staff would have great difficulty in coping with the increased demand. Additionally, they do not want to focus on chocolate alone because it is important that each member of the staff spends time working on a range of different products as this will enable them to develop a broader range of skills. South Hill Enterprise wants to grow the business, not to make money, but so that they can pay their staff higher wages and employ more people with disabilities. In effect, all of the primary goals are socially orientated rather than market-orientated. However, sales of the products are quite disappointing and there is little marketing being undertaken. A consultant is brought in to help but he quickly discovers that the usual business rules do not apply.

HYTEC (RICKIE A. MOORE AND OLIVIER TORRES)

Hytec is a small high-tech firm that was created by Jean-Jacques Promé in Montpellier, in the south of France. Hytec was his third attempt to launch a successful venture after being made bankrupt by the first two. Combining visionomics, electronics, informatics and robotics, Jean-Jacques developed a range of products that spanned three distinct market segments: nuclear, water treatment and offshore/oceanography. Hytec's products were both custom-built and standardised, and were sold and used worldwide from the inception. What began as a solo (micro) enterprise grew quickly into a small business. Hytec was driven by Jean-Jacques' never-ending passion for innovation and technology, and its success was arguably the result of its solid entrepreneurial foundation, leadership and strong innovation. Selling his shares so that he could retire, Jean-Jacques handed over the reins to Pierre-Emmanuel Gaillard, whom he had hired and trained. Pierre-Emmanuel realised that Hytec was approaching a critical point in its history – exports had been increasing steadily since 2000 and now accounted for 66 per cent of Hytec's annual sales (driven primarily by Hytec's constant innovative activity), the cost of sales was rising and the majority of its sales force did not belong to Hytec. With an exhaustive and impressive range of innovative products, Pierre-Emmanuel wondered whether it was time for Hytec to make a quantum leap and adopt a global entrepreneurship approach to its technology and innovation.

Contributors

THOMAS M. COONEY

Tom is Director of the Institute for Minority Entrepreneurship, Research Fellow at the Dublin Institute of Technology, President-Elect of the European Council for Small Business, founder and former chairman of INTRE (Ireland's Network of Teachers and Researchers in Entrepreneurship), a member of the European Commission Expert Group on Entrepreneurship Education and a member of numerous governmental advisory groups. He is a former Visiting Research Scholar at Babson College (US) and at the University of Durham (UK), and currently Visiting Professor at Turku School of Economics (Finland). He has lectured, researched and published widely on the topic of entrepreneurship, including *New Venture Creation in Ireland* (with Shane Hill, Oak Tree Press, 2002) and *Irish Cases in Entrepreneurship* (Blackhall Publishing, 2004).

ALAIN FAYOLLE

Alain Fayolle is a professor and Director of the Entrepreneurship Research Centre at EM LYON, senior researcher at CERAG, University Pierre Mendès France of Grenoble (France) and Visiting Professor at Solvay Business School (Belgium) and HEC Montréal (Canada). His current research works are focusing on the dynamics of entrepreneurial processes and the social effects of entrepreneurship education programmes. Alain's last published books were *International Entrepreneurship Education: Issues and Newness* (with Heinz Klandt, Edward Elgar Publishing, 2006) and *Entrepreneurship Research in Europe: Outcomes and Perspectives* (with Paula Kyrö and Jan Ulijn, Edward Elgar Publishing, 2005). Alain is also the editor of *A Handbook of Research in Entrepreneurship Education* (Volumes

1 and 2) and the author of a research-driven book, *Entrepreneurship and New Value Creation: The Dynamic of the Entrepreneurial Process*, both of which will be published in 2007, by Edward Elgar Publishing and Cambridge University Press respectively.

MARTINA JAKL

Martina is a partner with SwissCzech, a business consulting firm in Prague. From 2001 until 2006, she was a research and teaching assistant at the University of St Gallen. Martina holds a Masters in Management Sciences from the University of St Gallen and she is currently completing her PhD studies at the University of Economics in Prague. Her research interests include academic entrepreneurship, technology transfer and the internationalisation strategies of SMEs in Eastern Europe.

BENOÎT LELEUX

Dr Leleux is the Stephan Schmidheiny Professor of Entrepreneurship and Finance at IMD (Switzerland), where he is Director of the MBA programme and Head of Research and Development. He was previously Visiting Professor of Entrepreneurship at INSEAD (France) and Director of the 3i VentureLab, and Associate Professor and Zubillaga Chair in Finance and Entrepreneurship at Babson College, Wellesley, MA (USA) from 1994 to 1999. He obtained his PhD at INSEAD, specialising in Corporate Finance and Venture Capital. He is a specialist in venture financing, combining expertise in entrepreneurship, venture capital, private equity and growth management.

SOPHIE MANIGART

Sophie Manigart is a full professor at the Department of Accounting and Corporate Finance at Ghent University and partner of the Vlerick Leuven Ghent Management School. Her research interests are entrepreneurial finance, including the supply side (venture capital, business angels, stock markets) and the demand side (entrepreneurial companies). Her research has been published in books and journals like the *Journal of Business Venturing, European Financial Management, Entrepreneurship Theory and Practice, Small Business Economics* and *Venture Capital*. She is actively involved in managerial initiatives in the area of entrepreneurial finance, was founder and director of the Belgian business angels network

(BAN) Vlerick BAN, and is still director of BAN Vlaanderen. She is a member of the investment committee of Baekeland-fund, the risk capital fund for spin-offs of Ghent University.

DAVID MOLIAN

David Molian has been involved with entrepreneurship education at Cranfield University since 1998. Having trained in consumer goods advertising, he has been personally involved in the founding and sale of three businesses. David has served on the faculty of Cranfield School of Management, the Tanaka Business School, Imperial College, and as Visiting Professor at INSEAD (France) and London Business School. He has written widely on the marketing issues faced by owner-managed and growing businesses. David was educated at the universities of Oxford and Aix-en-Provence, and holds an MBA from Cranfield School of Management.

RICKIE A. MOORE

Rickie is an associate professor of Entrepreneurship at EM LYON and an associate researcher in the Institute for Socio-Economics of Organisations, both in France. He combines academia, consulting and research, and works and publishes in the domains of new venture creation, business development, organisational performance, performance measurement and management, and management consulting intervention methodologies. Internationally trained and educated, Rickie holds visiting teaching and research appointments in several universities around the world. A former chair of the Management Consulting Division of the Academy of Management, and active in several international networks in entrepreneurship, business and management, Rickie conducts intervention research in several firms worldwide and also serves on the boards of several firms and international organisations.

JOACHIM SCHWASS

Joachim Schwass is Professor of Family Business at IMD (Switzerland) where he teaches Family Business and Entrepreneurship. He is the director of the programme "Leading the Family Business". His main teaching focus is on owner-related issues and, in particular, from the next generation perspective. He has lectured and conducted family business programmess around the globe. He was educated in Germany, France and Switzerland. He has attended graduate studies at Technische Universität Berlin and Université de Fribourg where he obtained a Lic.rer.pol and a Dr.rer.pol. Professor Schwass has published widely, including the book *Wise Growth Strategies in Leading Family Businesses* (Palgrave Macmillan, 2005).

CHRISTIAN SERAROLS

Christian Serarols is a senior lecturer within the Business Economics Department at Universitat Autònoma de Barcelona and a member of the research group in "High-Tech Entrepreneurs in Catalonia". His research interests include entrepreneurship and small business management, eBusiness and electronic commerce. Christian has an industrial engineering background and a PhD in Business Economics, with industrial experience in technical research, consulting and management. He has founded a high-tech enterprise in the field of content aggregation.

JANE SILVER

Professorial Fellow Dr Jane Silver has lived and worked in a number of countries in Europe and worldwide. Since entering the field of education she has led a number of projects, mainly related to making the "world of work" more real for students. She regularly visits Finland as a visiting lecturer and has been invited as a guest speaker to a number of European universities, delivering lectures on working across cultures. As the Professorial Fellow in Enterprise Education at the University of Salford she develops enterprise teaching throughout the university. She is the course director for the Master of Enterprise programme.

KENT THORÉN

Kent Thorén has been involved in entrepreneurship for about a decade, both as a researcher and as a practicing entrepreneur. He has an engineering background, but his professional career has always been primarily oriented toward commercialisation issues and the development of new businesses. In 2007 he received a PhD in Industrial Management at the Royal Institute of Technology in Stockholm. He teaches Strategy and Entrepreneurship at this institution, and is also an acclaimed consultant in Strategic Business Development. His academic contributions provide ideas about entrepreneurial opportunities, motives for corporate ventures, growth strategy and growth management.

OLIVER TORRES

Olivier Torres is an associate professor at EM LYON, France and a specialist in small business management. He is the French Vice-President of the European Council for Small Business (ECSB), and Secretary of the International Francophone Association of Small Business and Entrepreneurship (AIREPME). His most recent book is *Wine Wars: the Mondavi Affair, Globalisation and "Terroir"* (Palgrave Macmillan, 2006).

JOSÉ MARÍA VECIANA

José María Veciana is an emeritus professor within the Business Economics Department at Universitat Autònoma de Barcelona (UAB) and has held a chair in several institutions, such as the European Council for Small Business. His research interests include entrepreneurship and small business management, eBusiness and electronic commerce. Dr Veciana has been the dean of the UAB and holds a PhD in Business Economics, and also has wide industrial, consulting and management experience.

THIERRY VOLERY

Thierry Volery is a professor of Entrepreneurship and Director of the Swiss Institute for Entrepreneurship and Small Business at the University of St Gallen, Switzerland. From 1999 until 2002 he was a professor of Entrepreneurship at the EM LYON Business School, France. He was previously a senior lecturer at Curtin University of Technology in Perth, Western Australia. Professor Volery serves on several editorial boards, including the *International Small Business Journal*, the *Journal of Enterprising Culture* and the *International Journal of Educational Management*. He holds a doctorate in business economics and social sciences from the University of Fribourg, Switzerland. He is the author of *Entrepreneurship and Small Business Management* (Second Pacific Rim Edition) (John Wiley & Sons, 2007).

French Art of Living

ALAIN FAYOLLE[1]

Fabien Deschamps and Jean-Paul LeClerc met while studying for their MBA. As part of their studies, they have being working on a new venture creation project and are now considering turning the project into an actual business. The basic idea is to start a restaurant chain based on an innovative concept mixing wine and cheese, and promoting the "French art of living". They want to launch a first restaurant in the Lyons area in France. Lyons is the second town in France after Paris (located in the south near the Alps) and it is recognised as a leading gastronomic centre in France. The potential founders have about twelve years of experience combined as senior executives in large companies and they have just completed an MBA. They have jointly designed their project and worked on the business plan which has just been presented to a jury as part of their final exam. They now have to make a definite decision – whether or not to start the business.

BACKGROUND

Fabien and Jean-Paul met at the start of an MBA programme in a French elite business school. As part of this programme and after attending a seminar on new venture creation, they worked in different teams to evaluate and present new business projects. Fabien's idea of a gastronomic restaurant was retained by his group, which worked on it for a week. Following on from this, Jean-Paul teamed up with Fabien and they worked together on this restaurant idea for about a year in order to turn it into an actual new venture project.

Fabien is 35 years old and married with three children. He has a degree in engineering (specialising in the food industry) and a postgraduate masters from a French business school. He has held managerial positions mainly in sales and marketing in large food industry groups where he has been able to progress quite quickly. Fabien also has a variety of skills. From a technical point of view, he has a good command of business-to-business and business-to-consumer marketing techniques, and of negotiations related to the sales of large-scale consumer products. His international experience has given him skills in international development strategy. He sums up his experience-based philosophy as follows:

> I know where I'm going, how I'm going to get there, how I'm going to get in, and what structure I should put in place.

Finally, Fabien has developed skills in managing sales teams and "how to drive and keep a sales team motivated". His responsibilities as a managing executive and board member in a large food firm have given him experience in general management and corporate strategy. Fabien himself describes the outcome of his professional career:

> Working on the board of a large international company is for me a great achievement. What it tells me is that I've progressed quickly, strongly and always in a correct and honest way, without stepping on the toes of other people! I am quite proud of this.

> I have made it because of my hard work. This means that I've sacrificed a number of things that I don't want to sacrifice anymore. For example, quite simply, my children: I haven't seen them growing up. I also realise that I've damaged some of my health. I have had a very serious health problem that came close to being a total catastrophe. I am therefore a little burnt out, not only from a health point of view but also intellectually. What I am trying to say is that there is a little voice in my head telling me that I don't want to go on like this. Another little voice is saying that it is fine but that I have three children to bring up.

> Looking back at my upbringing, the only goal was to succeed. If today one said to me "erase everything and tell us what you really want to do", I couldn't do it. Today we are in France, in a system where everything is linked to your degree and I am stuck with it. The fact that I have done an

MBA is a result of that logic. The only way to break out from this logic is to start my own company.

There is also the human element: relationships. I've now been taking a break for a year and finally I realise that my career path doesn't really reflect my personality. What I mean is that the path I took did not enable me to share what I like doing with others. At this point of my life I feel that my true personality comes out, but not in my professional life.

There are jobs for workaholics; there are jobs where you sleep badly, where you are constantly under stress. Myself, I was like that. I couldn't disconnect. I continued working when I got home. And there were weeks when I constantly worried because I was involved in difficult negotiations, because there were 20 or 30 million euros at stake and because on top of it, other people's work was at stake…. And if you lost the market, people could find themselves laid off, etc.

Jean-Paul is 38 years old and is also married with three children. He is a computer engineer and most of his professional experience comes from sales in the IT (information technology) sector. His professional experience has been mainly in large IT firms. The first one was HP for 18 months in New York. Then Jean-Paul joined his wife at Lille, a town in northern France where he was employed by Bull. A few years later the couple were transferred to Paris, where they spent four and a half years. Jean-Paul, his wife and their three children have now lived in Lyons for over six years. After Bull, Jean-Paul became a sales engineer for Sun Microelectronics. Taking advantage of a restructuring plan, he decided to leave the company and complete an MBA. Among the different skills acquired during his professional career, Jean-Paul numbers the total command of the sales approach, business-to-business marketing, sales, negotiation, networking and international experience as the most important. He feels he is autonomous, and has a feeling for communication (within a team and as a manager) and business commitment. Jean-Paul particularly emphasises his skills in developing new business:

I've especially had to develop new activities, and do business by creating my own network and by establishing contacts and partnerships.

The assessment that Jean-Paul has done of his track record and experience also highlights a certain dissatisfaction in terms of his career:

> I realise today that if I don't do this project with Fabien, if things turn out differently, I would like to take up a position as senior management. The reason is that I have lived with different management styles and with various people working around me, and there was often a problem of values. I've worked in both a French company and an Anglo-Saxon company and I saw management errors after management errors. Not necessarily in terms of strategy but rather when it came to people management. I've seen a lot of managers building their personal network without being particularly interested in others, neither personally nor professionally. They are permanently covering their own back and not showing any real leadership. This is something I find difficult to live with.

> I believe that work ethic is important. For me, you have to put a lot into your work and do things well. People should progress according to merit and not according to connections. I would like to build something based on people and not only on procedures.

THEIR PERSONAL AND FAMILY ENVIRONMENT

As a person, Fabien sees himself as an "introvert", someone who has difficulty having a natural, easy contact with people. This personality trait would also be visible in his professional behaviour. To "reload his batteries", he likes to be on his own. Wine is one of his great passions and he spends a lot of time taking part in wine tasting events, visiting vineyards and looking for the best wines to buy. He also reads a lot and his second great passion is nineteenth century literature. Finally, Fabien loves sailing and other water sports. He has a real passion for the sea, which allows him to both "share things with his friends and family and escape on his own". Fabien has travelled extensively and has taken part in a number of trade fairs. He has, as a consequence, developed an extensive network of professional and personal contacts. Fabien's education has always focused on achievement:

You should constantly try to finish in the best possible position. You spend your time constantly trying to prove that you are better than the others and it wears you out.

Regarding his family, Fabien mentions two types of behaviour. On one hand:

My parents are all but entrepreneurs. They are both employees who have climbed the career ladder with tenacity, with their diplomas, and with their work. There aren't any real entrepreneurs in my family. They are all people who have been very successful in life but as employees.

However, on the other hand:

My wife connects me with another dimension. It's the complete opposite in her family, where there are only entrepreneurs, particularly in the catering business where they have been quite successful. On that side of my family there are two extremes: there are those who today are between 60 and 70. They are from the old school, who took risks to succeed and in getting out at the right time. To be more specific, 80 per cent of the catering business in Toulouse (a medium-sized town in the south of France) is in the hands of my wife's family. There is also a relative of my wife who today is the director of a large Parisian tourist establishment. He really is one of the top managers today and uses the most modern and sophisticated methods of management and administration. To summarise, I have great admiration for these people who have managed to build something quite extraordinary starting from nothing.

Regarding his close friends, Fabien defines them as:

People who have exactly the same professional background, I mean they are about the same age as me and have the same profile as Jean-Paul! We have more or less all succeeded within large companies, progressing rapidly and taking on a lot of responsibility. In addition, we all have several points in common. We like eating well and sharing certain things. We all have three or even four children.

Jean-Paul spends a lot of time with his family and friends. Watching movies, reading, doing activities connected with wine and running are his main activities outside of work. His wife is a chemical engineer. She began her career at Unilever and within a few years had progressed into the purchasing area. Jean-Paul has always considered earning money as a success indicator, even though he has only progressed a little in this respect:

> Well, what has driven me up to now has been money, obviously. For me, money was the evidence of success. Someone who has succeeded is someone who has accumulated as much money as possible, who earns a good living and makes it clearly visible to everyone, etc.... Today, I'm past that stage and I want to do simple things with my family and close friends and not drive myself mad any more.

Jean-Paul's parents have a family business. They did not study much and started to work very early. His father was a sales representative in the paper trade. He took over one of his client's companies. Jean-Paul's mother joined him and took charge of the accounting. They developed the company over twelve years and then sold it. After that, they bought a café/restaurant that they still run today. Jean-Paul's sister is a lawyer. She was part of an independent law firm. She sold her client portfolio to another lawyer, left and went to Houston (USA) where her husband had been transferred. In his family, there are several manufacturers, some millers and other craftsmen who are involved in Armagnac in the southwest of France. The couple's friends are mainly engineers, executives or managing executives in large companies. Some run small- to medium-sized companies.

IDENTIFYING AN OPPORTUNITY

The concept Fabien and Jean-Pierre defined came from a simple observation. As France is known for the quality and variety of its wine and cheese, an alliance between wine and cheese appeared inevitable. Recent studies had shown that each of these two markets, wine and cheese, are quite dynamic. The latest studies from the dairy products trade association union point out that the consumption of cheese in France is increasing, with new trends developing around three concepts:

- **Pleasure**, which is characterised by sweet, fruity flavours, wavy and creamy textures, and exotic aromas (e.g. cumin and spices).

- **Authenticity,** a value strongly connected with cheese, is symbolised by the region or the "terroir". It is distinguished by the AOC and AOP[2], traditional production, and by wooden packaging. The return of traditional recipes like "tartiflette" (a dish made with potatoes, bacon and cheese) and "truffade" (a dish with truffles) has also been observed.
- **Diversity:** the consumption of cheese is no longer confined to the end of the meal. People can eat cheese at different points of time during the day and during a meal.

These changes in eating habits therefore offered new opportunities within the cheese market in France.

At the same time, a study carried out in September 2003 by the French statistics office, entitled "French People and Wine: Usage and Attitudes", was published. It was based on a representative sample of the French population aged 18 years and older. The study indicates that even though the consumption of wine in France is decreasing, it is becoming more and more a passion and a pastime for people. Consequently, products of a higher and higher quality are being bought. Consumers drink less often but look for quality wines, original, well processed and matured, and collect more and more information regarding the type of vines used, the area where it is produced and the aging process. This has resulted in recent years in an increase of small local wine merchants responding to these new niches. However, even though the number of places and opportunities to discover and try cheese or wine is multiplying, consumption outside the home, paradoxically, remains completely disassociated from it. It was within this context of change in eating and drinking habits that Jean-Paul and Fabien thought about a new concept: why not create a place where cheese and wine become the main ingredients of the meal, a place where the customer can discover all of the varieties, wealth and complexities of these two products; or a place where consumption can evolve through a modern approach to labour and quality?[3]

THE CONCEPT

The concept defined by Jean-Paul and Fabien is an alternative to traditional restaurants, based on the development of an association between flavours and aromas, and on the assembly and presentation of original, high-quality cheeses, and their relationship with wine. It would be a meeting place where as a customer you would engage in a real journey throughout the world of cheeses and wines, which act as the main ingredients of the meal.

It is not just about their taste. Advised by high-quality staff, you discover their wealth and variety, and learn more about how wines and cheeses fit together. The idea behind the venture is to offer a new way to enjoy wines and cheeses concurrently. Jean-Paul and Fabien want to modernise gastronomy, mixing new original recipes with traditional ones, letting guests explore all of the strengths and complexities of these flavours. The setting would encourage an atmosphere of sharing experience, where the service alternates subtly between recommending the product and managing the sales process. The decoration through a collection of supports (accessories, menus and so forth) should arouse curiosity and foster sales. The surroundings will encourage this extended discovery to be continued beyond the meal itself. It would be an area of leisure where guests can take advantage of the French Art of Living, where food should be savoured slowly and in the company of good friends. During this journey, the guests will experience real emotions and leave the establishment feeling that they have experienced something quite unique.

The business will be based on the one hand upon the organisation of events (e.g. the arrival of the new springtime Comté cheese, specific recipes, the discovery of a producer who comes to the premises to present his products and how they are made, or an area of production, tasting and sampling evenings, etc.), and on the other hand upon a menu that is constantly modified (at least every season). The menu will be based on the associations of new aromas and products associated with original cheeses (an example is "Argan" oil[4] on dry goat's cheese). These two approaches should allow the business to attract and retain a base of loyal customers. It would be a luxury environment, refined, private but modern, where the materials chosen will enable the lovers of wines and/or of cheeses to experience them pleasantly and comfortably in a calm atmosphere, and to discover the hidden secrets of cheese and wine. Beyond the pleasures of the table, entertainment will be provided enabling the customers to feel free from the restriction of time and to prolong their evening well beyond their meal. It will also be a delicatessen, where guests can take away a cheese tray presented in the form of a cleverly chosen journey of taste. There will also be a cellar where they can buy the wines that they have discovered and have them stored on site if they do not have an appropriate cellar. According to Fabien and Jean-Paul, if the first location is a success, then the ambition is to develop a chain of restaurants possibly through franchising. The plan is to start restaurants in France, as well as to engage in an international expansion.

EMERGENCE OF THE PROJECT

Fabien is the initiator of the project. He has been considering this idea for several years:

> The idea came about four or five years ago. It was linked to two things: wine and cheese. It is a real passion. However, I think that what really kicked off the idea was when we decided, in my last job, to launch a new brand of pasta. It included the development of a concept restaurant that we opened in Place de la Bastille in Paris. We defined a very detailed concept, lamps for example above each table in the form of eggshells, and I think this process was a revelation for me. I realised that there was something that could be done in this area.

The choice of sector seemed natural to Fabien, as he has always been involved in the food industry, both during his education and in his professional life. While Jean-Paul would have been more at ease if the idea had been to create a service company, this was something that did not interest Fabien. He always had inside him the dream of creating his own company:

> To create my own company; I've always had the idea, always wanted to be my own boss. Moreover, I nearly did it when I finished my engineering degree. One of my wife's uncles was a cheese wholesaler and suggested that I take over his company. I analysed the financials and studied the project in detail but then I became frightened and didn't want to take the risk. Although this person was going to help me, I was only 22 and I felt that it was too much for me to take on.

Jean-Paul also likes the idea of creating a company, but his motives are less clear:

> Creating a company, for me, has for a long time meant the peak of success. Not necessarily for me, it's really a general point of view. I've always admired entrepreneurs more than ÉNA[5] graduates.

RESOURCES AND ASSETS THAT CAN BE MOBILISED BY ENTREPRENEURS

The two entrepreneurs have worked hard to develop their personal network within the catering profession. They have the support of the Institut Paul Bocuse and of the Lyon Hotel School.[6] A first draft of their business plan has been written and they now have to contact potential investors. The founders intend to register the name that they have chosen for their company quickly, but it has not yet been done. On this subject Fabien admits that:

> Since the project was presented in October, we haven't made much progress. But we've got everything we need; it's just a question of launching the project.

Fabien is well connected in the catering sector, which allows him to consider the next steps with confidence:

> Today I've got doors that are open everywhere. The only door that remains closed is the investors but that's because we haven't tried to open them yet. My father is a banker so this should help me. I've also got another asset that I haven't used yet – it's my trump card – all my in-laws are involved in catering businesses. This should be of great help.

Jean-Paul agrees with most of this analysis and concludes:

> I think that with Fabien we have developed a good network. We already had a basic network thanks to my parents. Even though they experienced ups and downs, after so many years they now know the profession well. We can rely on them for some recommendations and advice in order to be able to get to understand better some key aspects of the business. On Fabien's side there is also a very good network, mainly among his in-laws. In addition we have developed a very useful network together, both on the company creation side and with the Institut Paul Bocuse, and as company founders in the catering sector I think that we have followed the right path. We'll see. We've met people. I think that we should really be able to use this network! We've met a lot of professionals who

can give us help and advice. So, for the activity that we have chosen to work in, I believe that we've got a solid network.

The two entrepreneurs appear to have a number of useful skills and resources to start their business. They are both prepared to invest €60,000 each in the project. However, they state clearly that they do not feel ready to put their personal assets at risk, for example, in Jean-Paul's case to mortgage his house. In their view, they lack two important resources today, which are operational experience in catering and the necessary financial resources to develop the concept further into a possible franchising concept. Regarding the issue of financing, Jean-Paul points out:

> Today, we probably lack credibility in the eyes of investors. So it's really this area that we'll have to work on. On the other hand, for the rest, if we manage to raise enough funds, I think that in operational terms, we'll have some really quite strong assets when compared with other founders.

Fabien points out the specific aspects of the profession that interests them:

> There is this operational aspect that I don't fully command today and of course it's not really something that attracts me. It is not a question of going to a guest table and talking about wine. That is what I want to do. But to go to a table as a waiter, to serve the plates, well, this really isn't my thing. I would be ready to make some concessions for a while but it is definitely not my thing. This means in concrete terms that there is a resource problem today. We need another person to join the project. We could create a special structure. He would have, if necessary, a majority in the pilot project to keep him interested. We know perfectly well that there are plenty of very competent people in this business who dream of just one thing, to start their own restaurant. The idea that appeals to me is to replicate the concept. So we need to set up something so that this person can manage the restaurant on a daily basis and that Jean-Paul and I can go on to the next stage of validation of the pilot project and start expanding. What really interests me is to develop the concept in France and abroad, as well

11

as to manage the entire structure, and in particular the brand. The initial stage doesn't interest me very much.

The lack of operational experience in the catering profession is therefore leading them to look for a partner competent in this field. They explain it in the following way:

> Today we're at the same point; we need a third operational person. We have identified certain people. We're in a phase where everything is a question of opportunity. For example we met someone a couple a days ago who is back from England. Last week we saw someone else, and then we also met a master cheese maker. The ideal would be to find now the third person (who wants to be in on this project) but we have not found him yet. We need a person who would be capable of managing the restaurant on a daily basis according to our views, while we manage the support function and focus on activities beyond the restaurant.

The addition of a third person, a catering or restaurant professional, is leading Fabien to think about another initial organisational structure:

> Ideally, if I look at the situation, I would have a back-up job that would allow me to have a guaranteed income, that would allow me not to take too much income from the company for the first two or three years. It would also enable me to live correctly. Today I know exactly how much I need to do this. It would help me to manage the gap between the end of my regular income in June and the launch of the business at the earliest in September. The key is to find the third person.

As a consequence, Fabien hopes to find a job in his current hometown, Lyons, a job he describes as an "income" job. He links this job to the restaurant project:

> This job should enable me to go to the restaurant as often as possible, to support the manager, to relieve him from some tasks that I can do well, so that in two years, if it's a real success in terms of sales, we can start expanding and

earn royalties. Then I'll stop the first job. Moreover, if I can go to catering schools, business schools or institutes like the Institut Paul Bocuse for training, then it would be ideal. Today it's extremely complicated for me; it would be an interim solution. I certainly do not want to put the project on hold. I realise that if I abandon this now, I'll never do it. It is now or never.

THE VIEW OF THE SPOUSES AND RELATIVES

Those close to Fabien and Jean-Paul have different opinions about the project. Fabien's wife openly encourages him to make this move: "If you think that it will be good for you, go ahead!" His close friends are generally positive, both about the project in particular and the type of career move in general. The two eldest children of Fabien also support him, while his parents express considerable caution and would prefer that their son went back to his previous position: "It is completely mad, go back to your thing, go back to what you know."

Jean-Paul's wife and his children's young age seem to pose more problems. When considering his children's education, Jean-Paul's wife would like to devote more time to it. On the other hand she is at the moment reconsidering her own career development. Jean-Paul summarises this by saying that:

> I think it's the current situation that poses a problem. If I would take a job today, it would make it possible for her to stop, to spend time with the children, to cope with the changes, and to think about what she could do or would like to do. Well, today she's a purchasing manager; she's got experience and good references. Perhaps she could work in consulting, but to do that she would need to be comfortable with everything else.

Jean-Paul and his wife are also having more trouble than Fabien and his wife regarding risking part of their personal assets:

> And then, there's something else. It's managing the risk. Today we've got a house that is fully paid. We don't want to mortgage it and put our standard of living at risk. We have become too accustomed to it. Putting this at risk is

not what we want to do! Where we are prepared to take risk is in our future projects, not in what we've built so far. We don't particularly want big cars. Camping holidays or things like that are enough for us. We simply need an income that will enable us to keep this standard of living, to educate our children, to take them out, to take them away on trips maybe once a year, to broaden their minds, that sort of thing; to help them when they start out. Today we can manage all this.

If the family and those close to Jean-Paul were interested in the project right at the beginning, their vision and perception have become less positive since. This is particularly the case of Jean-Paul's wife:

At the beginning she said to herself, "Look, he's trying to find himself" and by gradually recognising the drawbacks that this job would mean, she has ended up being frightened of the project.

Only Jean-Paul's father-in-law still finds the project interesting and supports him. Jean-Paul's parents had for a long time kept their opinion to themselves and he never knew anything about it until his sister told him:

Listen, they don't dare to talk to you about it too much, but Mum and Dad are quite worried. They've been working as their own bosses for a long time and they're getting more and more fed up with it. The fact that you're thinking of doing the same thing upsets them.

QUESTIONS STILL UNANSWERED

Today Fabien and Jean-Paul consider that a sufficient number of aspects have been dealt with to validate their catering concept. Well run, the business should be successful despite the risks, particularly as the financial structure was planned with the help of experts, which should help minimise the risks. But there is no such thing as a no-risk business. Fabien expresses his convictions:

I personally think that we've got a project that is well designed and its validity is confirmed each time we have a meeting with professionals. It's a project that I strongly believe in because traditionally, for the French people, wine and cheese is what they really like, and if it's managed properly, if we bring in conviviality and a good atmosphere, and if we can adapt to what they are looking for each time, whether it's learning or celebrating.... Yes, I'm very optimistic. I tell myself that it has to work. I don't want to abandon it because I am 100 per cent convinced that it has to work. If we can locate it in the centre of Lyons, it's going to be a great success, I'm absolutely certain of it, totally convinced. And you know people can sense that I believe in this project. I've seen it. It shows!

But uncertainties and question marks still persist. They are first of all personal, in terms of family and work in general. Fabien explains them like this:

Clearly my personal aim is to raise my children safely and soundly in every respect: personal fulfilment for each one of them, achieving their goals, and quite simply from a financial and health point of view. This is very clear. From a very personal point of view, considering myself, I am sure that I no longer want to live with the same level of stress. And it's a very important point, I've stretched myself hard in several directions in the past, it's going to be difficult for me to find a solution. I've got a very clear view of the last part of my life. I love the sea and my aim is to have a house by the sea with a boat in front and to be able to enjoy my grandchildren. This is very important and above all I have no intention of going through the hell that I experienced a year and a half ago, with the conditions I had to face when I left my last job.

For Jean-Paul, it's more of a spiritual quest for change in his personal and professional life:

I realise that situations are rarely simple. We have so much heritage from our parents, our experiences. It is difficult to come to have a clear view and for it to be complete. There is something to find, your way in life to find. I don't know whether I admire it or find it stupid, people who are very clear about their life very early on and know what they've got to do, but I think that we all need each other for help to be able to progress. And so, I'm interested in listening to others for my own benefit, as well as helping them.

Jean-Paul also has question marks linked to his wife's position:

> Well, my wife is wondering about her activity, she has other things she wants to do. So there is that as well. And, I think that if I commit to a thing like this, in any event, for two or three years, until things take off, she'll have to continue in the same activity as now and for the same level of income. I think that she has other ideas. She wants to do something else, something that would bring in less money. Finally during all my MBA this year, she had to deal with a lot and she really looked after everything, even though she had just begun a new job and had a lot of work. She saw me take a break and I think she would like to take one as well. Then to tell her, after working hard for a year and a half for my MBA, to tell her that I'm starting something else for another year and a half, two years up to my ears in work to get something going, this, I think is going to be a problem.

The two founders are stressed by the fact that they will not have any income in six months time, once their unemployment benefits have stopped. For this reason Fabien and Jean-Paul are looking for jobs at the same time as they continue with the development of their project. For example, Fabien stated that:

> My education has been one of my greatest achievements and helped secure everything. But today, I feel totally insecure, and for as long as my search for a new job continues I will feel insecure, and I don't like it at all. I know perfectly well that if I go and see investors for the project I won't be any good, they'll notice, I won't be able to lie to them.

Questions are also raised regarding the sector of activity:

> The catering sector is known for being really difficult. It is true that when we meet people, they tell us that investment is not that common, because there are a lot

of failures. It's also a difficult sector because in terms of hours, there are drawbacks that are really exceptional, difficult to balance with lifestyle. In addition, in terms of staff, everyone says that it's difficult to find good staff and to keep them. So, it's a profession that presents a number of difficulties. And then, it's a profession that I've never worked in, where there are a large number of clients to cope with, influential people who are not at all like those in the business-to-business sector.

WHAT TO DO NEXT?

The final uncertainty that came up recently refers to the founding team and their increasingly divergent views. Jean-Paul summarises their last conversation:

> Recently Fabien and I had a discussion about what we wanted to do, what our attitude was, and our levels of commitment. I confirmed to him that I didn't want to be part of the everyday work in the first restaurant. He said to me, "Ok, now we have to decide, do we go on with it or not. We cannot do things in half measures". I replied that I needed a little more time to reflect. "If you want a reply, if you are asking me to commit now, I understand your position, but if you want something that is clear now, the answer is no! Because I cannot say yes to you in a definitive way" and so I confirmed my position to him which was to say that it was also going to depend upon my wife, on how she saw things. And then I said to him, "Ok, listen, the only thing that I'll commit to you today is to go to the investors with you", and at this point he said to me, "If you don't want to come, I'll go on my own". I said to him, "Fabien, if you want to go on your own, the only thing I can commit to now is to give you my time, to help you because I like the project, and if I am available, I will go with you to meet the investors". So, we left it like that, and then he said to me, "Listen, things are clear, that suits me, I'll continue with all this" and we told each other that we'll do this at the same time as looking for a job.

Appendix 1A: **Background to the Sector**

Political Context
Social regulations in France aim at enabling the catering and hotel sectors to become more attractive, thereby attracting people to work in them, while maintaining considerable flexibility for the owners in terms of working hours for their staff, something that is essential for the success of such businesses.

Economic Context
Catering is very sensitive to the economic cycle and to household confidence (it is one of the first types of expense people decrease when times are difficult). In fact, thematic and gastronomic catering generally takes the brunt of an economic crisis (for example the 2003 recession). In addition, price increases in the average bill boosted by the switch to the Euro have hidden the difficulties of a sector that has lost 10 to 12 per cent of its customers (especially in the evening).

Social Context
The customers are continually evolving in terms of needs and expectations. They switch more and more and like to discover new things (new atmospheres, new flavours). They are more and more concerned about their health, eat less but choose quality products, and drink less alcohol but look for higher quality. There are currently two main types of expectations related to catering:

- The "nutrition" meal (generally at midday), associated with very good value for money and quick service, while at the same time remaining balanced and healthy.
- The meal "for pleasure" when the client is looking for something new. In that case, originality, the surroundings, the atmosphere and the quality of service all play an important role.

In recent years, the greatest successes in catering have been based on the concept of "leisure" catering, where the meal is actually a pretext. The restaurant then becomes "the pre-discotheque" place, up to two o'clock in the morning, or even a direct competitor to the discotheques and all-night bars. Therefore the successful interaction among the clients, the central theme of the restaurant, and staff who are highly qualified and who know the products perfectly, could become key success factors in the years to come.

Intensity of the Competition
The strengths of the industry are analysed as follows using Porter's model:[7]

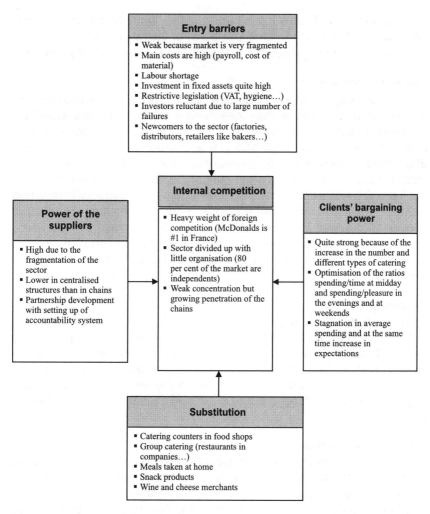

Entry barriers
- Weak because market is very fragmented
- Main costs are high (payroll, cost of material)
- Labour shortage
- Investment in fixed assets quite high
- Restrictive legislation (VAT, hygiene…)
- Investors reluctant due to large number of failures
- Newcomers to the sector (factories, distributors, retailers like bakers…)

Power of the suppliers
- High due to the fragmentation of the sector
- Lower in centralised structures than in chains
- Partnership development with setting up of accountability system

Internal competition
- Heavy weight of foreign competition (McDonalds is #1 in France)
- Sector divided up with little organisation (80 per cent of the market are independents)
- Weak concentration but growing penetration of the chains

Clients' bargaining power
- Quite strong because of the increase in the number and different types of catering
- Optimisation of the ratios spending/time at midday and spending/pleasure in the evenings and at weekends
- Stagnation in average spending and at the same time increase in expectations

Substitution
- Catering counters in food shops
- Group catering (restaurants in companies…)
- Meals taken at home
- Snack products
- Wine and cheese merchants

Source: Fabien and Jean-Paul's business plan

The Wine Market

The main producers are the famous vineyards, the wines cooperatives and independent small producers. The structure of the distribution in France gives a strong leadership to the GMS system (mass-market distribution through hypermarkets and supermarkets). However, other actors, such as wine merchants and wholesalers, play a role.[8]

The Cheese Market

In this market, we find three categories of producers: industrial cheese dairies, cooperatives and small producers. The offer is concentrated and the main competitors appear more and more as large companies. Also in this market, the distribution is largely in the hands of the GMS system. Other distributors hold marginal positions. In the beginning of the twenty-first century the total production in France is just over 1,000,000 tons.[9]

The Bread Market
For French people, bread has always had a very strong evocative power. In the course of time a truly affectionate relationship has developed between consumers and bread and it is not about to disappear. French people consume on average 153 grams of bread per day as opposed to 900 grams in 1900, although consumption has stabilised. 98 per cent of them eat bread every day, 74 per cent of the items bought are baguettes but there still exists 80 varieties of regional loaves and special loaves (with walnuts, raisins and rye) that are increasingly sought after. Here again, consumption is going towards quality products that retain all their flavour and crispiness, as well as towards more diversified and original products. The production and the main channel of distribution come from the traditional bakeries.[10]

Substitution
Despite the launch by large and medium-sized retail stores of special publicity events in their shops and the offer of in-company catering at midday, the greatest threat comes from the wine and cheese merchants. They organise meals and theme evenings either on their own or with restaurants. However, this substitution remains weak in the sense that it does not go beyond their usual product range, is not well structured and is occasional (entertainment).

Internal Competition
In commercial catering, the underlying trend regarding meals outside the home is represented by an increasing proportion of the households' overall food budgets. This proportion was 10 per cent in 1965 and 16 per cent in 1980. In 2000 it went up to 20 per cent. Commercial catering attracts 75.8 per cent of this budget. 120,000 players share the catering market. In terms of size, organisation and administration the players are very mixed. 80 per cent of the turnover is achieved by independent establishments. Their turnover is €25.8 billion. The other establishments are part of large companies and have a turnover is €11.9 billion. The restaurant chains represent only 4 per cent of these establishments but generate 20 per cent of the total commercial catering sector turnover. Their success is due to their modern organisation in terms of marketing, their sales power and their superior position in the sector.

The product types offered by catering fall into six main categories:

- theme catering
- classic catering

- gastronomic catering
- cafés and restaurants
- snack bars
- fast food catering

These catering categories have quite different trends. *Fast food catering* is booming because it corresponds to changes in society where saving time is a constant priority. However, it is very volatile because it has to be permanently in touch with clients' changing rewards. *Traditional and gastronomic catering* is stagnating as a result of weak profitability (104,000 establishments, average turnover is below €300,000, excluding VAT). In addition, the product that they offer no longer meets new consumer trends. *Theme catering* – entertainment, destination – is having a growing success that can be explained by the fact that going to a restaurant is increasingly viewed as a leisure activity. However, this area of catering is the one most sensitive to changes in household confidence. Moreover, innovations have trouble surviving beyond the fashion or novelty effect. A seventh catering type, *catering delivered to the home*, is showing significant growth since it corresponds to the changes in current lifestyle. In fact, the increasing French custom of "snacks" is becoming more and more beneficial for catering sales outlets in public places (shops, museums, etc.).

Catering remains a very competitive sector that for a number of years has been going through a crisis period that can be explained by two main factors. Firstly, a staff shortage of both skilled and unskilled positions, as well as staff who often lack motivation and give poor service. Secondly, a lack of confidence that has developed with consumers as a result of a number of food scandals, particularly related to BSE, that have led clients to turn to fresh, quality products (with labels showing origin). The key factors of success in catering are *quality and good value for money* aligned to the concept developed and the target market, the *location* that determines the visibility of the establishment and that corresponds to the catchments area, the *service*, atmosphere, decor, welcome, conviviality and originality of the concept. The decor and a pleasant atmosphere help to create the soul of the establishment. It so happens though that every study shows that the best advertising medium for a restaurant is word of mouth. *Consumer confidence* is essential at the same level as *management factors* such as marketing, stock, staff management and income management.

Analysis of the Key Success Factors of Direct Competition
Competitors can be assessed according to the criteria that contribute to their success: location, menu, atmosphere, perceived quality, image, sales approach, support and client relationships. The "gastronomic" type is linked to the pleasures of eating, the quality of the ingredients and how it is representative of the French culinary heritage. The criteria used to

evaluate those establishments are the qualification of the product (variety, quality, freshness, origin of the products, tradition, compliance with rules and regulations, etc.), the quality perceived (also including how the products are laid out, the presentation, and the attitude of the staff), the image of the restaurant within these gastronomic or even artistic aspects, and finally the support.

The "entertainment" aspect focuses on "fun", a change of scenery or destination. The aim is to offer a complete night out. The meal becomes a pretext; the atmosphere and the decor are the ingredients for success. The criteria used to evaluate those establishments are more linked to the atmosphere (particularly the change of scenery through entertainment, attitudes, events outside the norm and the unusual feeling of discovery, even surprise, and especially a lot of room for freedom so that everyone can enjoy it at their own pace), the image (but within its aspects of modernity, of the "current fashion", and of movement and enthusiasm), the sales approach (push and pull, public relations, personalising the rapport), support in its aspect of conviviality and good feeling, and finally in the efforts for interaction between the client and the concept, arousing curiosity and a reaction, the memory of having experienced an exceptional moment (the staff, entertainment and so on).

NOTES

[1] This case was prepared by Alain Fayolle of the Entrepreneurial Process Dynamics Research Centre, EM LYON, France. It has been prepared as a basis for class discussion rather than to illustrate either the effective or ineffective handing of an administrative situation. The author would like to thank Narjisse Lassas-Clerc (EM LYON) and Benoît Gailly (Université Catholique de Louvain, Belgium) for their help.

[2] « Appellation d'Origine Contrôlée » and « Appellation d'Origine Protégée » are two labels guaranteeing the quality, origin and authenticity of a product

[3] A detailed sector analysis is given in Appendix 1A.

[4] Argan oil is a Moroccan traditional oil coming from the argan tree. It has a nutty flavour.

[5] The "École Nationale d'Administration" (ÉNA) or European School of Governance is one of the most well known French elite schools. It was created by General de Gaulle to train the best students for positions at the highest executive levels of government services.

[6] Both schools are well known with a high reputation in the catering world.

[7] Porter, M. (1982) *Choix stratégiques et concurrence: Techniques d'analyse des secteurs et de la concurrence dans l'industrie,* Paris: Economica.

[8] More detailed information about the French market could be obtained from some websites: <http://www.montpellier.inra.fr> or <http://www.secodip.fr>.

[9] Ibid.

[10] For more detailed information, see the website of SOFRES, the French statistical institute: <http://www.sofres.fr>.

IViewCameras

DAVID MOLIAN[1]

In early September 2002, Pete Rankin walked out of his Planning Your New Business presentation at Cranfield School of Management, feeling a mixture of anger and disappointment. His business plan to sell wireless CCTV (closed-circuit television) cameras over the Internet had just been torn apart by the adjudicating panel. Among his fellow students Pete had been hot favourite to walk off with the prize for the best plan. He had put huge amounts of effort into preparing his presentation. Yet the feedback from the panel had been quite negative. Where had he gone wrong? Was he kidding himself that there was a successful business here to be built? Or should he remain confident in his own judgment and ignore the views of professional investors?

BACKGROUND TO PETE RANKIN

Pete Rankin would probably agree that he was destined to be an entre-preneur. Born in England in 1969, by the age of only six he had set up his first entrepreneurial venture with his brother, selling painted fir cones by the side of the road when on holiday in the USA. Pete continued to demonstrate entrepreneurial tendencies throughout his teenage years and while still at university set up and ran a business selling old-fashioned red telephone kiosks to collectors. Upon graduating in 1992, Pete entered the world of advertising. For the next eight years he worked his way up through the ranks as an account executive, moving from one agency to the next in search of promotion. Between 1997 and 1999 he spent two years in Cape Town, which gave him a lasting taste for Africa. He then returned to the UK to take up a position as group account director.

Still not thirty, Pete was doing well by the standards of the advertising industry. His next logical career move would be to join the board of a significant advertising agency. However, he remained bitten by the entrepreneurial bug and quit his position to set up a business of his own: an online art gallery. Unfortunately, the idea did not work. Forced to liquidate the company, Pete decided to take a career break and spent a few months touring Africa. In early 2001 Pete found himself reading a guide to business schools on the banks of the Zambezi River. It was at this moment that he made the decision to come back to the UK and do an MBA at Cranfield School of Management in the south-east of England.

Pete remained convinced that the way forward was running his own business and that business school would broaden his commercial experience and equip him with new skills and contacts. A year later, he was deep into his MBA and considering ideas for new ventures. One of his early ideas was to set up a luxury game farm in east Africa. As part of this, he was considering installing a CCTV system so that guests could see exactly what was happening across the farm in real time. In investigating this, Pete found some very impressive wireless CCTV products listed on Yahoo. This discovery led to the concept of selling CCTV cameras over the Internet and Pete spent the next few months with several fellow MBA students developing a business plan and undertaking research.

MARKET RESEARCH

Without doing any detailed research in the field, Pete established that the market for wireless CCTV cameras in the UK was just in its infancy compared with the USA and the Netherlands, where the market was much more mature, with many products and retailers. The closer he analysed the market, the more attractive he thought the opportunity looked. UK retailers actively selling CCTV cameras sold them either as a technology product (e.g. buy this Trust 100M Camera System) or as spying products (e.g. watch your neighbour). Only recently had high street retailers such as PC World, Homebase, Innovations and The Gadget Shop started to list wireless CCTV products, where they were positioned as marginal rather than mainstream consumer products.

His research also identified that the current products had functional, aesthetic and technological weaknesses. User-friendly and functional software for remote viewing over the Internet was not available yet, although technically feasible. Some information about the size of the market for CCTV and other electronic security related products was available, but Pete could not find anything specific about the UK market for wireless cameras. Instead, Pete had to work with fairly generic data about markets for substitute products such as baby monitors, conventional (wired) cameras, access control systems, camcorders and 3G mobile phones' video transmission.

THE OPPORTUNITY

The opportunity Pete envisaged was to create a brand – IViewCameras – to market CCTV cameras based on customer benefits, not on technology. The business would sell peace of mind (*not* a security camera), and would package the remote Internet viewing product so that it was exceptionally easy-to-use and install. This would give Pete an edge over his competitors.

Based on advice from a Cranfield faculty member, Pete began to sell wireless CCTV sets to other people on his programme (as well as one to his mother). This was extremely helpful in obtaining feedback from their usage of the product. The fact that he was able to sell some products to fellow MBAs proved that his product was attractive even to people with no money! Pete saw opportunities for IViewCameras in several markets:

- **BabyView** Camera: parents monitoring babies/children
- **DoorView** Camera: security-conscious consumers monitoring front doors
- **SecurityView** Camera: home and car
- **RemoteView** Camera: option to view a remote location via an Internet connection
- **PartyView** Camera: consumers wanting to view and record parties, adult entertainment and so on.

When asked some time later about what additional market research he wished he had done, Pete confidently said:

> None! Small enterprises cannot afford to waste money doing market research. It is cheaper and simpler talking directly to the customers instead and to start selling to them on a small scale.

A POSSIBLE PARTNER

The Cranfield MBA programme had several courses dedicated to entrepreneurship, which create the opportunity for MBA students to meet entrepreneurs and hear their stories. One of these entrepreneurs was a Cranfield MBA alumnus called Nigel Apperley and Pete made his acquaintance in April 2001, when Nigel came to Cranfield as a guest speaker. Two years before, after being made redundant, Nigel Apperley had set up InternetCamerasDirect (ICD). ICD was an Internet retailer dedicated to selling digital cameras and related accessories. In the time between setting up ICD and presenting to the 2001/2002 MBA programme, Nigel had turned ICD into the UK's biggest online digital cameras retailer, taking over half the online market for digital cameras.

Pete was impressed with Nigel's presentation and it got him thinking about how he and Nigel might work together to get the wireless CCTV idea started. He researched the digital camera market just to get a better idea of the size and trend for his own business idea (see Table 2.1 below). A couple of weeks later, Pete was in a bar one evening on campus, discussing the idea with his fellow students. In walked Nigel with a friend and sat down at another table. Pete decided to take the initiative and went over to Nigel to show him the products he was selling and to discuss his idea. At first, Nigel was not interested. He had seen CCTV cameras and felt that at £400 they were too expensive for what they were. When Pete told Nigel that he could get them for £40, Nigel suddenly became very interested! The two of them spent the rest of the evening discussing what a partnership would look like and came to the conclusion that sharing infrastructure would be a good way forward. The conversation ended with Nigel suggesting that Pete come to his office a few weeks later to present his idea more formally.

Table 2.1: **Digital Cameras Market**

	units, 000s	Index	RSP[i] £m	Index	Average price per unit £
1997	60	100	18.8	100	313.3
1998	170	283	72.8	387	428.2
1999	320	533	126.2	671	394.4
2000	610	1,017	165.0	878	270.5
2001	1,000	1,667	215.0	1,144	215.0
2002 (est)	1,250	2,083	250.0	1,330	200.0

[i]RSP = retail sales price

Source: *Mintel Cameras and Digital Cameras* report, April 2002. Reproduced with permission.

A POSSIBLE DEAL

Two weeks later, Pete presented Nigel with a hardcopy of a PowerPoint presentation and an outline business plan (the executive summary from a revised version of this plan is given at the end of the case as Appendix 2A). Nigel was very impressed with Pete's energy and enthusiasm. Pete liked Nigel's operation and wanted to close a deal there and then. Although Nigel was impressed with Pete, he wanted time to think about the deal and to run some numbers. He also had a couple of concerns. First, the plan envisaged that Pete would be starting up the business with others from Cranfield, both as shareholders and managers. Nigel wondered why Pete needed so many friends involved in the business. Nigel had discussed this issue with a Cranfield lecturer who was supporting Pete and the lecturer agreed. From a business perspective, he too could not see why Pete needed so many people. Second, Pete wanted to develop his own products and to contract out production as well as be a retailer. Nigel, however, felt that he should stick to being a retailer.

INTERNETCAMERASDIRECT

At this time (quarter two, 2002), ICD was on target to turn over more than £13 million for the year, double the sales for 2001. Nigel was confident that the business would continue to expand rapidly as the market developed and digital cameras became a mainstream consumer product. Nigel had based the business in an old manufacturing town called Marsden, near Manchester, 250 kilometres north of Cranfield. An Internet-based business could operate more or less anywhere and Marsden had a number of advantages:

- It was where Nigel and his wife were living before Nigel lost his job
- It was an area of low labour cost and (relatively) high unemployment
- As an old woollen mill town, Marsden had a good supply of redundant industrial buildings available to rent at a good price

Still the majority shareholder, Nigel had built ICD through an excellent website, with good customer service and strong branding. He had also been very astute in gaining trading agreements with both leading manufacturers and wholesalers of digital cameras. Now that the market was taking off, these were much more difficult to obtain, and so constituted a barrier to new entrants. At the moment ICD operated on tight margins and was still consuming cash, although Nigel felt that this situation would change as the business reached better and bigger economies of scale. Draft ICD financial statements for 2002 are shown in Appendix 2B.

From Pete's point of view, ICD had substantial benefits to offer:

- A picking, packing, and posting operation
- A credit card fraud detection process
- A website infrastructure
- An accounting infrastructure
- A large balance sheet for negotiating terms for credit and discounts with suppliers
- A marketing team
- A database of 33,000 existing customers with thousands more to come
- Cheap deals for credit card transactions

Perhaps most importantly, Nigel's knowledge of how to run a successful Internet business would be invaluable, not least knowing how to get your company's name high on the search engine lists without paying an extortionate price.

In exchange, Nigel felt that here was a good opportunity for him as well. ICD could benefit from:

- An equity stake in Pete's business
- A contribution to its overheads
- The chance to establish a related operation at very low cost
- Access to Pete's ideas for building an Internet business – applied to ICD!

THE DEAL

By midsummer Pete and Nigel came to a broad agreement that would form the basis of the relationship:

Shareholding
- ICD would receive an allocation of 200 out of 1,000 issued shares, for £2,000. The majority of the balance would be held by Pete, and a small percentage split between Cranfield colleagues who had worked on the project so far.

Products

- ICD would be used to purchase all IViewCameras' (IVC) products.

Marketing

- ICD would provide prospect and customer email addresses.
- ICD would provide prominent banner/hyperlink opportunities, and ICD sales staff would mention IVC at the end of order and contact emails.
- ICD would provide support for other online marketing, such as search engine positioning, reporting, etc.
- ICD would provide the opportunity to include promotional material in its product fulfilment packs.
- IVC would test market an affiliate programme.

Website

- ICD would provide the creation, hosting, updating and maintenance of the website.

Administration and Fulfilment

- ICD would ensure accounts support, to include VAT (sales tax) returns.
- ICD would handle all inbound enquiries and orders.
- ICD would provide fulfilment at an agreed cost per product of £7.50 for fulfilment and order processing, made up as follows:

  - Picking: £0.54
  - Packing: £1.62
  - Materials £0.10
  - Courier: £4.50
  - Administration: £0.74

- ICD would provide order processing.
- ICD would allow the use of their merchant agreement (for credit card payments).

EARLY DAYS

Peter and Nigel attended the first supplier meeting together. Nigel taught Pete a few tricks in handling suppliers so that he would be able to obtain good terms, including using Nigel's balance sheet as a negotiating tool.

By now it was August and Pete needed to have the website developed and live. However, this did not go smoothly. Pete was still doing his MBA, and was struggling for time. In addition, Pete had doubts about whether he was ready to commit to IViewCameras, since he was presented with several opportunities to earn large sums of money by working for other people. Nigel sensed this hesitancy and decided to put pressure on Pete to commit one way or another. Accordingly Nigel gave him an ultimatum, and told him that he needed to start making sales. Pete responded well to this pressure and had the website up and running before he finished his MBA.

THE PNB PRESENTATION

Pete had developed his thinking and his business plan for IViewCameras on a Cranfield elective course called Planning Your New Business (PNB), designed for MBA graduates planning to launch a new venture. This course culminated in a presentation to an outside panel at the end of August and Pete felt that he had made excellent progress. Most of his fellow course members were still at the planning stage. Pete, on the other hand, had now done a deal with Nigel. He had done some deals with suppliers and he had his website up and running. He had even made a few sales to impoverished MBA students!

He was confident in the business and was looking forward to post-MBA life when the course ended in September. He even found himself thinking that he was a contender to win the award for the year's best business plan (and Pete had never won an academic prize before). He put a huge amount of effort into his business plan and presentation. IViewCameras was by now well known across the School of Management and many people turned up specifically to see Pete's presentation of his business plan. In the plan, Pete was looking for £250,000 of external capital to develop the business, for which he was prepared to offer a significant equity stake.

Things started well but within the first five minutes of the presentation, Pete knew he had lost the venture capitalist (VC) on the panel, but he was not sure why. Once Pete had finished his presentation, it all became clear. The VC had already studied the plan and was not convinced. Specifically, he did not like the fact that Pete had developed a business model that involved being both being a retailer and developing his own products. He interpreted this to mean that Pete's ideas were unfocused. He had additional doubts about whether this business was sustainable in the long term, since there was no protection afforded by intellectual property or know-how that was difficult to copy.

Pete did not win the PNB prize. To make matters worse, after the presentation, one of the fellow panel members came up to him and told him that during the presentation he had taken his chequebook out and was going to invest in Pete's idea but once the VC started spotting holes in the business plan, he put his chequebook away again. Now he began to wonder if he should continue with the idea himself!

NOTES

[1] This case was prepared by David Molian, Visiting Fellow, Cranfield School of Management. It has been prepared as a basis for class discussion rather than to illustrate either the effective or ineffective handing of an administrative situation. The author would like to thank Peter Rankin and Nigel Apperley for their cooperation.

Appendix 2A: **Extracted from IViewCameras Business Plan: Executive Summary**

Currently IViewCameras Ltd directly sells easy to use, wireless colour video cameras, receivers and associated products used for monitoring your family, car, home or business. IViewCameras Ltd then plans to manufacture and directly sell/retail technologically advanced, functionally better and aesthetically superior wireless colour video cameras, receivers and associated products for monitoring your family, car, home or business. The wireless video cameras send colour or infrared black and white video pictures and audio wirelessly to your TV, video or PC (enables remote viewing via a website). Associated products sold include motion detectors, dedicated monitors (all sizes), remote video-recording products (which turn on the VCR to record for a set period of time or when motion is detected) and remote software for viewing pictures over the Internet.

The Target Markets
Parents monitoring babies/children (BabyViewCamera); security conscious consumers monitoring their front door (DoorViewCamera) or home and car (SecurityViewCamera); with the option of viewing via the Internet (RemoteViewCamera); and consumers wanting to view and record parties, adult entertainment, etc. (PartyViewCamera).

IViewCameras' Added Value and Competitive Difference
In the UK, wireless video cameras are just becoming available. In the USA and Holland there are many products and retailers. In the UK competitors are selling cameras as technology products (e.g. buy this Trust 100M Camera System) or as spying products (e.g. watch your neighbour). Current products have functional, aesthetic and technological weaknesses. Easy to use and functional software to remotely view over the Internet is not available but technologically feasible. IViewCameras will market the customer benefit proposition more effectively than competitors (e.g. selling peace of mind not a security camera), develop better cameras and package the remote Internet viewing product so that it is exceptionally easy to use and functional.

IviewCamera's Two-Stage Implementation Strategy

Development So Far: July to August 2002

- Joint venture with InternetCamerasDirect (20 per cent) set up, operational website live, sales have started, call centre and fulfilment systems are in place and £10,000 seed finance obtained.

IViewCameras

Stage 1: Direct Distribution of Existing Products – Objectives to March 2003

- Sell over 750 products generating approximately £70,000 sales turnover and approximately £14,000 gross profit by March 2003.
- Justify development and contract manufacture of "own brand" range and Internet software.
- Obtain business angel funding (£250,000) for product development.

Stage 2: Retail distribution and Own Brand – Objectives from March 2003

- Manufacture and launch "own brand/product" range and Internet remote access software.
- Sell approx 50,000 own brand products generating over £3,600,000 sales turnover and over £1,750,000 gross profit by 2006.
- Gain retail channel distribution and partnership agreement with a security organisation and telecommunications company.

IViewCameras – People

- Peter Rankin – Director, aged 32, has proven entrepreneurial experience having started two companies and nine years experience in direct marketing and advertising.
- James Marchant – Director, aged 27, has six years consultancy and marketing experience.
- Nigel Apperley – Investor, CEO InternetCamerasDirect: £20 million sales digital cameras website.

IViewCameras – Projected Financials Summary

Period	Volume	Sales	G.P.[i]	Costs	O.P.[ii]
July 02– March 03	755	£ 69,996	£ 14,308	£183,312	£(169,004)
Q2 03–Q4 03	3,500	£ 264,457	£ 127,957	£147,500	£ (19,543)
2004	11,250	£ 842,872	£ 404,122	£161,500	£ 242,622
2005	15,000	£1,123,830	£ 538,830	£122,000	£ 416,830
2006	18,750	£1,404,787	£ 673,537	£134,500	£ 539,037
Total	*49,255*	*£3,705,942*	*£1,758,754*	*£748,812*	*£1,009,942*

[i] Gross Profit

[ii] Operating Profit

Appendix 2B: **InternetCamerasDirect (ICD) – Projected Profit & Loss and Balance Sheets for the Calendar Year 2002**

Profit & Loss

	Debit	Credit
Turnover		£13 million
Cost of sales	£10.9 million	
Gross profit		£2.07 million
Distribution costs	£0.27 million	
Administrative costs	£1.67 million	
Operating profit		£0.13 million
Net interest receivable/payable	–	
Profit before taxation		£0.13 million
Dividends	£30,000	
Retained profit brought forward		£0.1 million
Retained profit carried forward		£0.2 million

Note: figures may not add to total, owing to rounding.

Balance Sheet

	Debit	Credit
Fixed Assets		£0.2 million
Current Assets		
Stocks		£1.5 million
Debtors		£0.6 million
Cash		£0.9 million
Creditors	£2.8 million	
Net current assets		£0.3 million
Total Assets less current liabilities		£0.5 million
Long-term creditors	–	
Called-up share capital		£0.001 million
Share premium		£0.3 million
Profit and loss account		£0.2 million
Shareholders funds		£0.5 million

Note: figures may not add to total, owing to rounding

NovoGEL

THIERRY VOLERY AND MARTINA JAKL[1]

Transforming starches into synthetic products has been a dream cherished by industry and science for a long time. The solutions up to now however have had one serious drawback – the products have not been waterproof. Rolf Müller and Federico Innerebner made a breakthrough, however, in the summer of 2001. With a special method, they were able to produce made-to-measure gels out of starch. This method is not only used to produce plastics which are impervious to water, but it is also a platform technology whose potential applications extend from the foodstuffs industry to medical technology. Furthermore, the technology works not only with starch, but with all other macromolecules. From the beginning, it was clear to Rolf Müller and Federico Innerebner that this would be the basis for founding their own firm. This platform technology brings with it a series of difficult decisions that have to be made. Which markets should be approached, and in what order? What should the organisational structure best suited for this look like? Both firm founders are materials engineers who do not have appropriate familiarity with and networks for every market at their disposition.

FROM THE IDEA TO ITS REALISATION

Synthetics play an important role in our daily lives, and their potential – in the opinion of many scientists – is far from being exhausted. At the same time, synthetics are much more than just plastic bags, but rather an economic material whose use is extremely widespread and that have many advantages. Synthetics, however, have a major disadvantage: they are produced for the most part from raw materials that are non-renewable (such as petroleum) and their recycling/disposal is problematic. Thus an intensive search for alternative sources has been made. For a long time

35

research in the production of synthetics from starch, a biodegradable and renewable raw material, has been underway. The solutions up to now have not been very convincing; in particular the solubility in water of these synthetics produced by starch turned out to be an extremely serious problem. Chemical modifications that make this sort of plastic water-resistant are indeed possible, yet these types of techniques are expensive or have produced unsatisfactory materials. A further variation is the physical combination of starch polymers, but here no important breakthrough had been made…up until a certain evening in 2001.

Rolf Müller and Federico Innerebner knew each other during their student days at the ETH (the Swiss Federal Institute of Technology in Zurich), where both of them had specialised in the subject of industrial materials. Federico Innerebner had always worked parallel to his studies and had even then founded two companies, including a firm concerned with wind energy. After receiving their diplomas as materials engineers, both of them were employed by their home university and then at Fluntera AG, a spin-off of the Zurich ETH, which in those days played a pioneering role in the field of developing synthetics from starch. And yet a basic problem could not be resolved there, namely the marked susceptibility of starch in relation to atmospheric humidity and water. The attempts at a solution carried out there by using chemical modifications or mixtures with water-resistant synthetic plastics also proved unsatisfactory, since the principal advantages of starch were thereby significantly reduced. After the Fluntera period, Federico Innerebner ended up in the private sector, where he was employed for several years at a large firm. Rolf Müller had been taken on at this time as a scientific collaborator at the Institute for Polymers at the ETH Zurich and concerned himself principally with research into the fundamentals and applications of starch.

The two gentlemen had little contact for many years, until Federico Innerebner called Rolf Müller in the autumn of 2001 about "some sort of equipment which was at the ETH". In the course of the conversation Rolf Müller mentioned to him that during his work at the Institute for Polymer Physics at the ETH Zurich in the summer of 2001 he had successfully been able to make starch completely impervious to water with a simple physical procedure. Rolf Müller had found a method by which macromolecules could be linked up three-dimensionally in a simple yet targeted way. No chemical additives were necessary for this; the procedure was instead based purely on physical principles. This procedure seemed to promise extremely good results since there were no additives, as had previously been the case, and conventional and inexpensive production methods could be used. Federico Innerebner immediately grasped the importance of this information. After the conversation he quickly drove from Uzwil to Zurich to see for himself. The samples that he saw in Zurich completely convinced him: samples of starch gel that had been immersed in water for several days were actually completely water-resistant. The mechanical qualities of these samples were no less amazing. It was immediately clear to both of them that this technology could be utilised for much more than just the area of synthetics and represented a unique opportunity. The pair's decision had already been made during the first evening: a new firm would be established.

This newly developed gel could be considered to be a genuine platform technology, since the method developed by Rolf Müller can be used for any sort of macromolecule. It can be specifically adapted to a particular purpose and utilised in diverse areas from medical technology to the foodstuffs industry. After they had protected themselves by obtaining a basic patent and by establishing the company in the second half of 2002, the question of how the company's founders should optimally market and secure this platform technology from a strategic and organisational point of view rapidly became applicable. From the very beginning, both excluded its marketing in the form of selling the patent, since they had both wanted to set up their own company using this technology. Their goal was the broadest possible application of the technology. The question was simply *how* this company could be optimally structured so as to operate successfully in a wide range of markets.

TECHNICAL BACKGROUND AND MAIN CONCEPTS

A *polymer* (Greek: polu – many; meros – part) is a chemical compound that is composed of chains of molecules or heavily branching structures of molecules (macromolecules). Polymers are mainly to be found in organic chemistry, and thus have a carbon basis, either as biopolymers (proteins, DNA or carbohydrates) or synthetic polymers (polyester, styropore, etc.), but there are also polymers, for example, which are silicon based (silicone).

Substances whose basic components are synthetically or semi-synthetically produced polymers are called *synthetics*. All synthetics are polymers, but not all polymers are synthetics. The vast majority of synthetic materials are produced from petroleum, natural gas or coal. The principal advantage is the inexpensive and simple processing. Yet the disadvantages are no less significant: the raw materials do not renew themselves and synthetic materials for the most part do not spontaneously decompose, or only after many years. Recycling has also turned out to be problematic, in order to improve the qualities of the materials a large proportion of the synthetic materials have to be used in combination with each other rather than using a single type.

Figure 3.1: **Schematic depiction of a physically connected network**

Figure 3.2: **Schematic section of a chemically connected network**

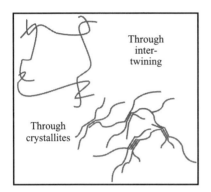

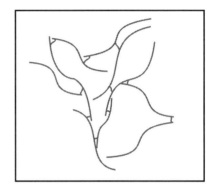

Gel describes a physical state which can vary between semi-solid and solid, and which can also be described as so-called semi-diluted polymer solutions. What is normally called gel (or simply "jelly") actually represents only one single aspect of gels. As shown in Figure 3.1 and 3.2 above, two types of gels are possible in principle: chemically and physically linked gels. Chemically linked gels are usually no longer reversible (i.e. they can no longer be returned to their original liquid state). Physically linked gels are reversible and are based on entwining or a mixture with crystallites. The mechanical characteristics of a gel can be determined by the network density, number and distribution of the connection nodes, as well as the proportions of the solution used. The full spectrum ranges from more or less solid bodies up to so-called hydrogels, in which the proportion of water can reach 99 per cent, which are familiar to the world as wound dressings.

Gelatine is a biopolymer which is obtained from animal by-products, and which can form a gel in combination with water. Classic uses for gelatine are in the foodstuffs industry (e.g. "jubes" (jelly bears), or for the clarification of soft drinks). Gelatine is also used in galenics as a material in capsules. In recent years, however, gelatine has come under heavy fire in connection with BSE and Creutzfeldt–Jakob disease. Gelatine not only has experienced problems because of BSE, but also because of continually recurring scandals involving spoiled meat, diverging dietary requirements and even regulations (vegetarian or kosher diets, to name just some examples). Even though the industry has insisted that industrially processed gelatine is harmless, this has not removed feelings of insecurity among consumers, even though consumers are not even aware that many products contain gelatine. A much more important aspect from an industrial point of view is the cost factor, since the use of gelatine in production is rather expensive, for example for soft capsules.

Starches (glucose polymers or so-called polysaccharides) are mainly familiar to us from the realm of foodstuffs – to thicken a fondue, or perhaps to make fish sticks crispier. Up to 40 per cent of starches, however, are also utilised in the non-food sectors (e.g. in adhesives and lubricants and construction materials and cardboard). The advantage of starches is that they represent a renewable, degradable raw material, which is furthermore biologically unproblematic and has demonstrated a favourable ratio of energy use in manufacturing.

FIELDS OF APPLICATION FOR NovoGEL

In the opinion of the two founders of NovoGEL, the following four fields of application (foodstuffs, galenics, medical technology and biodegradable synthetics) are the most interesting fields for the utilisation of their technology. Further potential exists according to Federico Innerebner and Rolf Müller with regard to synthetic gels (gel for preventing the formation of scars) and also in analysis (carrier substances for DNA analysis).

Foodstuffs

In recent years, the food industry has become ever more dynamic. Meeting the continually changing customer demands has proved to be a challenge. Functional food or foodstuffs with fewer calories or fat, or with reduced carbohydrates, remain popular. The European and North American markets are considered to be saturated, and the manufacturers are thus transferring their attention to the "emerging markets". According to a study by KPMG, this industry is in the midst of a process of concentration and ever changing consumer habits. In such an environment, more flexible company structures and the ability to innovate will become preconditions for survival under tough competition.

The industry is, however, considered to be rather conservative and is dominated by a few large market leaders such as Nestlé, Unilever and Kraft Food. There are also many small and medium-sized firms that are leaders in niches or in regions. Downstream, the food retail sector is likewise subject to hefty pressure to cut costs and is characterised by tendencies towards concentration. In several countries, the retail sector is simply an oligopoly comprising of three or four big retailers (e.g. Migros, Coop and Denner in Switzerland; Carrefour, Auchan and Casino in France).

For NovoGEL, there are various sectors within the food industry in which their technology could be applied. One example is in the area of confectionery where starch-based gels could be utilised as the vegetal alternative to gelatine. Their qualities are at the very least equivalent to those of animal-based gelatine and are furthermore much more cost efficient in terms of their production. Previous vegetal alternatives to gelatine had the problem that the jubes which were made out of them stuck to teeth in a disagreeable way, while in other cases the sensation of chewing them was unappetising. Additionally, the distensile properties of jubes derived from starches showed a marked difference to animal-derived gelatine; the alternative from NovoGEL on the other hand can be adjusted to that of "normal" jelly bears.

A further use of the technology from NovoGEL is the so-called glycaemic index (GI). This represents a new classification of foodstuffs, which measures the dissolution of these foodstuffs in the body by means of the blood sugar level. A higher GI means a more rapid digestion in the body and therefore a feeling of being full which does not last very long.

Easily digestible and extremely popular foodstuffs such as white bread or cornflakes are characterised by a high GI and therefore can pose problems (e.g. prevalence of diabetes mellitus). Meanwhile, the "fibre-rich" healthy replacement products – for example muesli – are not very satisfying in terms of taste for some people. As shown in Figure 3.3, NovoGEL can vary the GI of foodstuffs based on starches or even consciously design them while the food retains the same taste, which was previously impossible to achieve.

Galenics/Pharmaceutical Technology

Galenics is the original term for pharmaceutical technology as a sub-sector of the pharmaceutical industry. This industry is also dominated by international companies, whose sales volume goes into the billions and which are driven by intense mergers and acquisitions. The principal firms in the pharmaceutical industry (Pfizer, GlaxoSmithKline, Sanofi-Aventis) have in total a market share of approximately 15 per cent. The sector is under enormous pressure to bring so-called "blockbusters" – medications with an annual sales volume of more than $1 billion – onto the market. Furthermore, cost pressure in the health sector is continually increasing and the market for generic drugs is taking off.

Figure 3.3: **Comparison of Dissolution of Cereals**

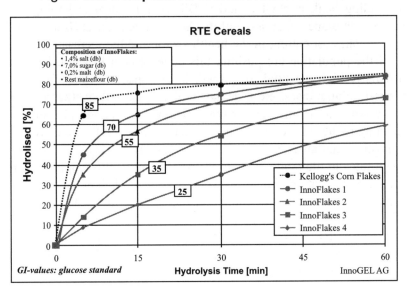

The pharmaceutical technology is almost exclusively concerned with the preparation of medical substances, which we know in their final phase as medications and thus almost exclusively with the production of drug forms. However, in order to be able to evaluate the effectiveness of medications, the administration form (that is galenics) must also be taken into account. There are liquid (e.g. syrup), semi-solid (e.g. salves) and solid forms (e.g. tablets) of administration. Capsules, as a solid presentation form, are composed of a gelatine covering, which encloses the active ingredient. The active ingredients can be present in the capsule in the form of powder, as a liquid or as a granulate. Through special galenic procedures tablets or capsules can be manufactured in such a way that a delayed release (retardation) of the active agent takes place. This takes place by means of wrapping particles of the active agent in film of varying thicknesses.

NovoGEL can position itself in this market with two applications: on the one hand the company can offer an inexpensive alternative to gelatine with so-called soft capsules; and, on the other hand, it can enable so-called controlled releases with its new technology. The active agent is thus uniformly released, the frequency with which the medications must be taken is reduced and due to the possibility of producing made-to-measure active agents the time of further release can be further refined. In both applications the convenience for patients will be increased.

Medical Technology

The leading bank in Switzerland (UBS) sees medical technology as a clear growth branch in an issue of its *Outlook* magazine (February 2005). In particular, cost cutting in the health sector and the increasing average age of the population are pushing this development forward. UBS sees particularly high potential for growth in orthopaedics (knee-/hip-joints, vertebral column/discs, etc.), dental implants, cardiology (heart/circulatory system, e.g. cardiac pacemakers, defibrillators) and ophthalmology (declining ability to see, due to age or diabetes), as well as picture-based diagnostics (digitalised x-rays). These markets are already showing annual growth rates in the range of 15 to 20 per cent and UBS's opinion is that there are no indications that this trend will come to a halt in the foreseeable future. Switzerland is furthermore considered to be one of the worldwide leading locations for medical technology and is comprised of some 500 companies with an annual sales volume of about 8.5 billion Swiss francs. Not only is the proportion of exports extremely high (90 to 95 per cent), but companies in the medical technology branch are considered to be interesting candidates for acquisition by the increasingly hard-hit pharmaceutical sector. With the NovoGEL technology, existing polymers such as polyvinyl alcohol can attain the qualities that are necessary for the markets mentioned above. Furthermore, the technology permits significantly simpler techniques in the operating room and thereby a shorter length of stay in hospital. This is a standard well attuned to an environment of cost cutting in the health sector.

Biodegradable Synthetics

Biodegradable synthetics were in fact the starting point for Rolf Müller and Federico Innerebner, and it is predicted that this material has great future potential within this market. While plastic can be counted among the most multi-purpose materials, the problems mentioned previously, such as recycling and disposal, cannot be neglected. At the moment, the annual growth in the synthetic market stands at about 5.5 per cent per year. The greatest share of production is held by plastic materials, whose main areas of application are packaging and construction materials. BASF has forecasted that the total world demand for plastic materials will grow by 260 million tons annually until the year 2010, with a higher than average increase in Asia. According to information from the branch association Plastics Europe, the EU holds a share of 24 per cent of world production at the moment, which is in the upper third, together with North America and Asia. In this branch, tendencies towards concentration and declining margins dominate as well. According to an estimate made by the branch association for biodegradable polymers, a market share of up to 10 per cent can be anticipated for biodegradable synthetics. In addition to ecological advantages, such products offer cost advantages also as their cost does not depend on the price of oil.

THE CHALLENGE

Rolf Müller and Federico Innerebner quickly became aware that with their findings they had platform technology in their hands. But the questions of *which* markets should be entered and *how* remained the main challenges. Neither financial nor personal resources existed for simultaneous entry in the market in all four fields. As the pair were at the start-up stage of their company, and are materials engineers, they did not possess detailed knowledge of and access to networks in these markets. It was therefore clear to the partners that they had to focus on one or two application fields. How the markets should be entered was also important since every market has its own particularities. It was important to the partners that the technology be utilised in the broadest possible way, and a necessary component of this included maintaining the greatest possible control over the technology. The firm's own "test kitchens", or laboratory, already existed and equipment at the ETH Zurich was able to be used. NovoGEL was also innovative in setting up their laboratory; among other things, NovoGEL was able to equip old refrigerators with worn-out cooling ventilators from PCs and a low-cost alternative to refrigeration units that would have cost several thousand Swiss francs was found. It was therefore possible to ensure rapid production of prototypes for the individual areas of business activity. Company representatives would be able to test the first samples of starch-based jelly bears for example. From a purely technical point of view, a market entry in various markets would be possible within a short space of time, but the company founders were not yet in a position to estimate costs for such an entry into the market.

NOTES

[1] This case was prepared by Thierry Volery and Martina Jakl of the Swiss Institute for Small Business and Entrepreneurship at the University of St. Gallen. It has been prepared as a basis for class discussion rather than to illustrate either the effective or ineffective handing of an administrative situation.

Beyond Products

SOPHIE MANIGART[1]

It was a sunny afternoon in May 2005. Despite the heat, Peter Van Riet was thinking of snow, snowboards and snowboard bindings. It took three years of his life and all of his savings to develop a revolutionary model of snowboard bindings. Having been a semi-professional snowboarder as a teenager, he sensed that the market was waiting for his ultimate snowboard binding. But he urgently needed money to start up a company, develop a first prototype, test it on snow and start sales and production, providing he wanted his first sales to happen before the winter season of 2006–2007. Four business angels were interested in his project. Together with his financial partner, Peter was considering how much dilution he would have to face for a proposed investment of €300,000 by a group of business angels.

BACKGROUND

Peter Van Riet used his knowledge of snowboard bindings and his training and experience as a product developer to design a completely new snowboard binding. His new binding combines extreme ease of use with the same freestyle feeling as traditional strap bindings. The current snowboard bindings are either strap bindings, where the boot is sealed by two straps, or step-in bindings, which can be compared to traditional alpine ski bindings. While being very versatile and adaptable to a large range of boots, a significant drawback of the strap binding is the fact that it is rather cumbersome to put on. To overcome this disadvantage, the step-in binding has been developed. The major disadvantage of the step-in binding is that is must be used with hard boots, which experienced snowboarders dislike, and it is more expensive than strap bindings. Snowboard addicts feel that soft boots are essential for the perfect feeling that is so important

45

in freestyle; moreover, it improves the comfort of the snowboards. Due to the disadvantages, the newer step-in binding has never taken over the dominant position of the strap binding. Meanwhile, a new company called Flow, which was established in 1996, introduced a different type of hybrid binding. Despite its non-natural way to step in and its limited ways to adapt the binding to the snowboarder, Flow rapidly became successful. The success of Flow suggests that the market is ready for a new product.

The new hybrid binding developed by Peter combines the ease of use of the step-in binding with the comfort of soft boots, without the disadvantages of the Flow concept. He further improved the comfort and flexibility of the binding through intensive co-development efforts with Italian and Belgian engineering companies, and with a major American chemicals company for the composite materials. This resulted in a hybrid binding, with the positive features of both the traditional strap and the step-in bindings. A first Benelux (Belgium, the Netherlands and Luxembourg) patent was filed in 1997 and expanded to the main winter sports countries in Europe, and to the US and Canada in 1998. No patent has been filed in Japan due to the high translation costs involved. The intellectual property protection expires in 2018. A first real test came when the hybrid concept was presented at the important yearly ISPO Trade Fair (the International Trade Fair for Sports Equipment and Fashion) in Munich in February 2001. Reactions were generally favourable for the new design and the concept proved to be on the right track.

Given that further development required more money than Peter possessed, he decided to involve a financial partner as a shareholder. However, the development proved to be rather slow and the financial partner eventually stepped out of the project, losing his initial investment. The product was further developed to the current "strap-in" binding that is now ready for full testing and, if technically successful, for commercialisation. Peter also sought coaching for the development of his business plan, something which he knew nothing about until then, by participating in a business plan competition, Bizidee. Not only did he win the competition in 2004, but he also found an experienced business partner with complementary financial and accounting skills willing to invest some money towards further product and business plan development. Together with the money, it was important that the new partner was willing to work part-time for the company.

Peter now feels that the business idea is sufficiently developed to start up a company, Beyond Products, which should be aimed at developing and commercialising the new snowboard binding. He has invested approximately €350,000 from his own, his first and his second partner's savings and time in the project up to now: €207,000 for the product development,

€81,000 for patent costs and the remaining for miscellaneous costs such as marketing expenses (mainly the trade fair). While the patent and marketing costs were out-of-pocket expenses, a large part of the product development costs consisted of his time. He estimates that Beyond Products needs €300,000 cash to get up and running, and to develop and test a prototype that could then be presented at the next ISPO Trade Fair in January 2006. This is essential, as orders for the 2006–2007 snow season are generated during the fair.

THE MARKET FOR SNOWBOARD PRODUCTS

Some 17 million snowboarders are active worldwide, accounting for one-third of the total winter sport population. Snowboarding is the fastest growing sport in the United States, with a yearly average growth rate of 11.4 per cent between 1988 and 2002. Half of all snowboarders are between 20 and 25 years old; 88 per cent are male. However, the number of female and of older snowboarders is growing steadily. The yearly average sales growth of worldwide snowboard bindings is almost 21 per cent since 1993, but it levelled off to a growth of 7 per cent in 2004. The snowboard industry currently represents about 15 per cent of all winter sport sales. Europe, the United States and Japan each represent approximately 30 per cent of the worldwide snowboarders' population. The remaining 10 per cent is active in Canada and South America. About 1.4 million snowboards have been sold in the 2000–2001 season, of which 420,000 were sold in the United States, 403,000 in Europe, 450,000 in Japan and 120,000 in Canada. Current worldwide sales of snowboard bindings are estimated to be 1.7 million. Not surprisingly, the Alpine countries – Switzerland, France, Germany and Austria – are the countries with the largest markets for snowboards and snowboard bindings in Europe. Independent industry watchers estimate that the traditional strap binding still represents 70 per cent of the market for snowboard bindings, the step-in binding has 20 per cent and the hybrid Flow binding 10 per cent (although Flow itself claims to have a 20 per cent market share). It is expected that the step-in binding will further lose market share to hybrid bindings. The step-in binding will therefore probably be repositioned as a more expensive niche product for the older, wealthier snowboarder.

Snowboarding is more than a mere sport; it is a lifestyle with its own code of conduct and norms. Image building is therefore the key when launching a new product or brand. Core snowboarders – the professional snowboarders sponsored by snowboard brands – are especially important in setting trends, which are then followed by the recreational snowboarders. It has happened on more than one occasion that a particular brand or product fails on the market if the core snowboarders do not endorse it. Furthermore, the lifestyle approach of snowboarders ensures that the major traditional brands active in alpine ski sports, such as Rossignol or Salomon, do not have the same dominant position in the snowboard market as they have in the alpine ski market. Snowboarders prefer smaller brands especially targeted towards the snowboard world.

A full range of snowboard products not only consists of equipment such as snowboards, bindings and boots, but also accessory apparel such as clothing, sunglasses and backpacks. The major players offer the whole range of products. The five largest companies (Burton, GenX, K2, Rossignol, Flow and Salomon) have 65 per cent of the market between them, while the next seven brands account for only 16 per cent of the market collectively. This makes the snowboard market very fragmented and leaves a lot of room for a large number of smaller and new brands. The major player in the snowboard bindings market is the pioneer, Burton, with an estimated market share of 24 per cent in 2002–2003. This company offers a full range of high quality snowboard products and actively sponsors a top team. K2 is the largest company active in the snowboard market with several brands (K2, Ride, Morrow and Liquid), together representing almost 20 per cent of the market. None of the other players have more than 10 per cent of the market.

A snowboarder is typically offered a choice of bindings separately from boards. A sport apparel shop sells both boards and bindings, assembling them on the site according to the customer's choice. There is hence no urgent need to team up with a snowboard manufacturer; marketing and sales of bindings occurs separately from that of boards. The average consumer price for a strap binding is €165, but prices range from €100 to €400 for top models. Flow sells its hybrid bindings from €170 to €340, with an average model costing €200. The average snowboarder becomes more demanding with respect to quality, design and comfort, making the top bindings more attractive.

THE FORECAST FOR BEYOND PRODUCTS

The mission of Beyond Products is to offer a range of high quality products that improve the comfort, pleasure and safety of snowboarders. The first product is the new hybrid binding. Peter forecasts that the new binding may capture 10 per cent of the worldwide market within seven years. The first sales are expected after the 2006 ISPO Fair, in February and March, and will be limited to Europe. Sales in the United States and Canada will start in 2007, and expand to Japan and the rest of the world in 2008. Taking into account a growing market, a growing market share and the introduction of new models and types, Beyond Products expects to sell 12,000 bindings in 2006, increasing to 280,000 in 2011. The evolution of the expected sales is shown in Appendix 4A. The sales price to the consumer will vary between €200 and €240, positioning the Beyond binding right under the top segment. This price will allow a gross margin of approximately €30 per binding for Beyond Products. Beyond Products intends to sell its bindings to importers, who then will sell them to retailers. The selection of European importers will happen on the ISPO Trade Fair in 2006, American importers will be sought on the SIA Snow Sports Show in Las Vegas in January 2007. Collaboration with existing brands selling complementary products may be sought in the future. Further, an international snowboard team will be sponsored from 2007 onwards.

The production of the bindings will be fully outsourced. If sales are generated in the first quarter of 2006, then production has to start in the second quarter of 2006. Launching a new product is costly, as it requires a lot of engineering and design, and an expensive mould has to be cast before production can start. It is estimated that launching a completely new model requires an investment of €200,000, a remodelling requires €125,000 and a different size of an existing model €110,000. The current product needs some further technical upgrading. However, preliminary testing of the concept has shown that it is technically feasible. A first important milestone will occur in December 2005, when a fully-fledged prototype has to be ready. It will then be tested on snow in the French Alps by Peter himself to test the safety of the product, and by professional snowboarders to test the technical qualities and comfort of the binding. A positive test is crucial in order to launch the binding on the January 2006 ISPO Fair. Missing that deadline implies missing a first year of sales.

The second important milestone is generating the interest of importers at the ISPO Fair, thereby generating sales in the first months after the Fair. If sales would be much lower than expected, the future of the company might be jeopardised. An alternative to the independent growth of Beyond Products might then be selling or licensing the intellectual property (IP) rights to an established snowboard company. Peter's dream, however, is to successfully launch the first product and to use it as a platform to build a new brand with a range of products, such as boots, backpacks, T-shirts, etc.

THE FINANCIAL PLAN

Appendix 4A shows the financial forecast as developed by Peter's partner. The plan takes only the sales of snowboard bindings into account, not the sales of other products that the company is planning to launch if successful. It is clear that €340,000 cash is needed in 2005 to set up the company and to develop and test the prototype. A further €500,000 is needed to fully launch the product in 2006, without taking financial costs into account. Peter estimates that the company will generate cash from 2007 onwards. Both profit and free cash flow are expected to be €4.4 million in 2011.

Beyond Products has already been awarded a subsidy and a subordinated loan by a government agency. The subsidy amounts to €65,364 and the loan amounts to €84,040. A part of the cash has already been used while some is still available in the company. The loan carries a yearly interest rate of 8.08 per cent and has to be repaid from 2009 onwards. Some market data has also been gathered. The yearly ten-year government bond rate was 3.26 per cent in the Euro zone in June 2005. There are few comparable companies in this sector that are quoted on a stock exchange that might yield comparable multiples. Appendix 4C shows multiples of some companies active in the athletic equipment sector. Finally, Peter wondered whether the announcement on 2 May 2005 of the takeover of Salomon (part of Adidas-Salomon A.G.) by Amer Sports Corporation would have an influence on the valuation. It has been announced that the take-over price (debt free and cash free) will amount to approximately €485 million. The exact price will reflect the net asset value of Salomon as of 30 September 2005, including €144 million goodwill. Salomon has net sales amounting to €653 million, gross profit of €259 million, and earnings before interest and taxes (EBIT) of €9 million (2004 figures). The Salomon EBIT figures include restructuring provisions of €19 million.

WHAT NEXT?

A syndicate of four business angels is interested in an equity investment of €300,000 in Beyond Products. This, together with a small bank loan, should allow Beyond Products to reach June 2006, when new cash (€500,000) will have to be raised in a second investment round. If the prototype works well in the "on snow" test and if reactions are positive at the ISPO Fair, then the new financing round could be done at much better valuations than now, as uncertainty will have been reduced significantly. Peter plans to transfer the IP rights, which are now in his personal name, to the company. Peter and his partner are currently considering how many shares the business angels should get for their €300,000 investment. But one of the key issues that they cannot resolve is what equity percentage would be fair to the business angels, without diluting the founders' position too much and also compensating them honestly for their efforts until now?

NOTES

[1]This case was prepared by Sophie Manigart, Professor at the Vlerick Leuven Gent Management School and Gent University. It has been prepared as a basis for class discussion rather than to illustrate either the effective or ineffective handing of an administrative situation.

Appendix 4A: **Profit & Loss Statement (€)**

	2005 (6 mth)	2006	2007	2008	2009	2010	2011
Sales (units)	0	12,000	57,000	126,000	200,400	259,675	286,081
Gross margin	0	354,960	1,719,781	3,877,654	6,290,663	8,314,369	9,343,040
Operational costs	-108,284	-560,560	-954,248	-1,386,229	-1,632,479	-1,806,973	-1,906,686
EBITDA	-108,284	-205,600	765,533	2,491,424	4,658,184	6,507,396	7,436,354
Depreciation	-27,644	-178,554	-338,580	-398,374	-433,423	-335,748	-332,749
EBIT	-135,928	-384,154	426,953	2,093,051	4,224,761	6,171,648	7,103,605
Financial costs	0	-29,771	-71,677	-137,719	-209,519	-266,705	-292,219
Taxes	0	0	0	-615,749	-1,402,426	-2,064,986	-2,376,124
Profit/loss after taxes	-135,928	-413,924	355,276	1,339,583	2,612,816	3,839,957	4,435,262

EBITDA: earnings before interest, taxes, depreciation and amortization

EBIT: earnings before interest and taxes

Appendix 4B: **Cash Flow Statement (€)**

	2005 (6 mth)	2006	2007	2008	2009	2010	2011
EBITDA	-108,284	-205,600	765,533	2,491,424	4,658,184	6,507,396	7,436,354
Investments	-238,635	-310,994	-639,473	-239,471	-237,487	-142,394	-641,802
Change in working capital	8,512	20,417	-25,370	-47,141	-73,709	-70,710	-32,213
Taxes	0	0	0	-615,749	-1,402,426	-2,064,986	-2,376,124
Free cash flow after taxes	-338,407	-496,177	100,690	1,589,064	2,944,562	4,229,305	4,386,216
Cumulative FCF	-338,407	-834,584	-733,894	855,170	3,799,732	8,029,037	12,415,253

EBITDA: earnings before interest, taxes, depreciation and amortization

FCF: Free cash flow

Appendix 4C: **Multiples of Quoted Athletics Equipment Companies**

Name	Exchange	PE	PBV	PS	EV/ EBITDA	EV/ EBIT	Firm Value/BV	EV/ Sales
HEAD NV	Vienna	NA	0.63	0.32	9.37	28.81	0.79	0.62
UMBRO PLC	London	17.36	3.83	1.22	8.99	12.16	2.50	1.49
AMER GROUP	Helsinki	14.23	2.07	0.83	7.57	10.47	1.78	0.96
PUMA AG	Xetra	17.74	8.31	2.50	10.43	11.21	8.00	2.36
ADIDAS-SALOMON AG	Xetra	20.18	3.87	0.81	9.78	12.89	2.51	0.97

PE: price/earnings ratio

PBV: price/book value ratio

PS: price/sales ratio

EV/EBITDA: enterprise value/earnings before interest, taxes, depreciation and amortization

EV/EBIT: enterprise value/earnings before interest and taxes

Firm Value/BV: market firm equity value/book value

EV/Sales: enterprise value/sales

Boblbee

BENOIT LELEUX AND JOACHIM SCHWASS[1]

The summer of 1998 would be one that Patrik Bernstein would never forget. One Friday evening, he sat in a small cottage in Torekov, southern Sweden, assembling some 200 backpacks with his partners, Sam Bonnier and Jonas Blanking, their wives and many friends. It was a world apart from his Indonesian ex-pat lifestyle with Unilever, but he was enjoying himself. On the Monday morning they had loaded three cars with the Boblbee backpacks and set off in three different directions – to Stockholm, Göteborg and Malmö – to deliver their first order to the Swedish sports retail chain The Stadium.

That first major delivery was a momentous step in the short life of their start-up company. When the three partners reconvened in Torekov a few days later, and the high had time to wear off, reality hit them – they had no clear strategic plan for the company. Their focus had been on finalising the design of a launch product and getting the first order delivered. With that done, what next? After a few hours of discussion, they elected to postpone any decision until after the International Trade Fair for Sports Equipment and Fashion (ISPO) in Munich, a major trade event scheduled to take place three weeks later, in September.

The response they received at the fair was sensational – everyone from competitors to media loved the backpack, the urban marketing brochure and Boblbee's unconventional stand. Marketing experts reckoned that the Boblbee backpack would be the next inline skate – it was revolutionary! The hype was totally unexpected for the company. As many as eighty-four distributors showed interest in distributing Boblbee. Bernstein said:

> We had rough price lists, but no real marketing plans – we were not prepared for this response. We sat in our hotel room after the first day, drinking whiskey, talking

about prices and strategy. Where should we position our-
selves? We knew our costs, but we had never discussed a
distributor pricing strategy. We had only produced a few
prototypes and made one sale. What distribution channel
should we be using? How should we organise production?
What should our proposition be?

GLOBAL ACT AB (GAAB)

Bernstein and Bonnier were old friends from when they had both attended the Sigtuna boarding school in Sweden for six years. Bernstein
commented:

> When you are at boarding school you develop a special
> bond, it is deeper than a normal friendship. You go through
> quite a lot together, and that stays long after graduation.

At the beginning of the 1990s, Bernstein started to feel restless in his
position as a "fast tracker" at Unilever. He had reached a point in his career
where he needed to be "re-energised" and to face new challenges and possibly less politics after some fifteen years in the corporate world. One long
summer's day in 1995, Bernstein and Bonnier sat in their bathing suits on
a cliff at Hallandsväderöarna on the west coast of Sweden talking about
life and what to do next. Neither of them knew that the other had plans to
start a business. Bernstein had only shared his plans with his wife so far,
fearing that he would not be taken seriously and also that someone would
steal his ideas. The two nevertheless opened up to each other and were
elated to discover that what they had in mind for their respective futures
was quite similar and fairly compatible.

Bonnier wanted to start a concept called "toy factory", while Bernstein
had dreamed up Spotlight (The Big Little Theatre) which was a way for
children to learn through the arts. It took only minutes for them to realise
that they would be stronger together, so they decided to start something
jointly. They invested equal amounts of money and set up Global Act AB
(GAAB) in Torekov, a small, sleepy summer town with great golf courses
and beaches on Sweden's west coast. For no particular reason, Bernstein
took the role of CEO and Bonnier that of Chairman. They wrote business
plans for both Spotlight and the toy factory, but in the end decided to do
Spotlight first (refer to Appendix 5A for a brief description of Spotlight).

BACKPACK ENCOUNTER

In 1996, during the development of the various technical components needed for Spotlight, the duo started to work with Swedish industrial designer Jonas Blanking. Bernstein remembered the first encounter with Blanking: "It was 'click' at first sight! We had so much in common and yet we were so different." It was during the first meeting with Blanking that Bernstein noticed a prototype of a mysterious-looking backpack hanging in Blanking's studio. However, it was not until Bernstein was trying to launch Spotlight in the US that he finally got a chance to experience the backpack concept. He was staying with one of Blanking's friends (Chet Swenson) who at the time was trying to sell the backpack concept to the sports manufacturer K2 as a licensed product. The hard, funky backpack was lying beside a bed in the guestroom and Bernstein could not help picking it up and playing with it. He was fascinated, but equally surprised that it was just lying around, so he asked Blanking why nothing was happening with the backpack. Blanking was a designer to the core and less of a businessperson. He had asked Swenson for help and Swenson had made a few attempts to present the pack to some bigger sports companies, but did not receive a positive reaction. It did not appear to appeal to them. Bernstein saw great potential in the concept and was also truly impressed with the work Blanking had done for Spotlight. Bernstein and Bonnier decided to suggest that Blanking become a partner in GAAB. The three of them could then develop a multi-brand strategy around Spotlight and the backpack.

In 1997 the three shook hands and GAAB was split in three equal parts and the backpack project was codenamed Boblbee, for Bonnier, Blanking, and Bernstein Enterprises (refer to Appendix 5B for the capital structure), and Blanking took over responsibility for product development. The company adopted an abstract of a person in freefall as a logo, symbolising Boblbee's soul – free!

THE GENESIS OF BOBLBEE

The original idea for the backpack had come to Blanking when he was riding to work, usually on his rollerblades or bike. He was tired of having his books, laptop, MP3 player, gym clothes and other bag contents destroyed by rain or shocks. So he started developing a novel backpack that would match his needs, which he assumed would also be those of his generation. To create a light, yet impact-resistant casing, Blanking looked mostly at the air cargo industry for inspiration. The industry handled many small shipments for which it used special containers that had to be light yet strong and protective. It quickly became clear that the keys to a successful new backpack were: (1) a sophisticated weight distribution system that would shift the effort to where it would be least felt and (2) the use of composite materials that would be both light and resistant. Blanking researched the plastic and aluminium structures used in air cargo containers to create the backpack structure and impact-protection casing. He also investigated how the containers were assembled, the types of screws used and how the materials reacted in various stress situations and corrosive environments. To make the backpacks comfortable, it was critical to use a soft harness, but combining the hard shell with the soft harness proved to be the most difficult part of the product development. Blanking produced several mock-ups and prototypes in 1996, which resulted in the first working prototype. Boblbee incorporated materials that had never been used before for backpacks. It combined a monocoque hard shell with a set of soft harnesses, in a unique, ergonomic and radical design. It was highly functional, with many pockets inside and add-ons that could be attached to the outside of the backpack for even greater usability and flexibility.

Boblbee was built around the following features:
- The Lumbar Support System™, which included the S-design that separated the upper load area from the lower lumbar support area. The Lumbar Support System ensured excellent weight distribution and reduced stress on the back.
- The Quick Lock and unique Bellow Flex™, which allowed easy access and flexible volume adjustment.
- The monocoque hard shell, which not only provided optimal Impact Protection™ for sensitive products such as laptops and cameras, but also protected its carrier.

The monocoque hard shell was initially based on thermoplastic injection moulding with materials such as ABS (acrylonitrile-butadiene-styrene terpolymer) and acrylic. This ensured high tensile strength, excellent thermal properties and flexible surface treatment. But the hard shell could be developed further. Materials such as recycled plastic, metals such as aluminium or titanium (radically new materials in the backpack market), and crystalline materials (such as carbon or Kevlar fibres for very high-end backpacks) could also be used. The surface materials could be changed or anodized, the colours could easily be altered and graphics such as logos and pictures could easily be added. For a true "street oriented" design, all it took was a couple of cans of spray paint. Various graffiti artists would be invited to customise the shells. The harness was made of several flexible foam plates that optimally followed the movement of the body. Each plate conformed to its own area, for example pelvis/hip, waist, shoulder blades and shoulders/arms. The inner structure of the harness was covered in DuPont 1000C Cordura, a synthetic high-performance fibre that ensured resistance even after years of wear and tear. The material was also water-proof. Countless hours were put into designing the assembly, primarily to find ways to hide all the seams to avoid fraying fibres. The external seams were sealed with Cordura-clad piping. Boblbee hoped to continue to work with agents at DuPont and in Hong Kong and Korea to make sure that the company always had the latest in fibre technology.

The nuts and bolts were essential pieces in the Boblbee system. They joined the flexible back plate to the hard shell through a watertight synthetic rubber gasket and an aluminium ledge. The nuts and bolts were also important for the add-on equipment and were designed to conform to specific attachments and strengths. The nuts and bolts were surface-treated to avoid corrosion, discoloration and material fatigue. Each Boblbee fixture was made up of a corrosion-resistant zinc and iron blend, with a super strong Deltacol black surface. The combination was tested in a salt chamber for 400 hours and showed the same corrosion protection as stainless steel, but was lighter.

PATENTS

A provisional patent application for Boblbee™ was filed on 6 January 1997. GAAB conducted two independent patent searches, one at the US patent office and the other at its Swedish equivalent, the *Patent och Registreringsverket*. The searches revealed no significant prior art for a monocoque three-wall shell and a flexible fourth wall. The patent lawyers saw the probability of getting a patent on these key features of the design as very good. During the summer and autumn of 1997 Awapatent (a Swedish company specialising in patent protection) prepared an international patent application and included ten areas of innovation. The PCT (Patent Collaboration Treaty) application was filed on 5 December 1997. The patent was expected to come through in autumn 1998, but in the meantime the hard shell of the backpacks was embossed with the inscription "Pat. Pend." GAAB also sought trademark protection for the Boblbee brand in all the markets where it planned to be active.

SUPPLY CHAIN

Considering the high-tech nature of the Boblbee backpack, and the multiple technical competences involved in its manufacture, it was clearly inconceivable to manufacture and assemble entirely in-house. There were a number of critical constraints. Firstly, it was important that all suppliers of the various Boblbee components were strong, established, quality-conscious and had leading-edge technology. Secondly, the company was quite open to forming partnerships with its suppliers in order to make the cooperation even more successful. One of the arrangements considered was to subcontract the entire backpack production to an equipment specialist, and to focus on the design, marketing and sales of the product themselves. This approach would require little financing upfront, but they did not have a subcontractor in mind. There were also concerns about quality control and potential conflicts when introducing further innovations, with the integrator possibly dragging its feet if faced with costly changes. Finally, with a technology product, it was deemed valuable to stay in direct contact with some of the manufacturing or assembly operations so that direct feedback could be established from marketing and sales. A second approach would be to source the components through reputed independent producers, but keep the assembly and final quality control in-house. So far, the shell and cleat were made by Nolato Termoform, a Swedish producer of polymer materials, and the nuts and bolts were produced by Willum Nielsen (a Danish specialty producer), Nedschroef in the Netherlands and Bufab Bix AB in Sweden. The harness was sourced in Asia, mainly China. The longest lead-time was for sourcing the harness, which could take up to three months. A potential production facility had been located in Torekov. It had a total area of 800 m^2, of which 160 m^2 was used for office space and the rest could be used for storage, assembly and despatch. The facility would have the capacity to assemble and ship up to 8,000 Boblbee backpacks per month, as well as several hundred Spotlight kits. Such an arrangement could possibly be further optimised by using suppliers on a global basis. They could also consider developing a number of assembly plants around the world.

MARKETING

After the product launch at The Stadium, GAAB decided to commission its first marketing brochure. One of Europe's best design photographers, who had also done shoots for the trendy jeans manufacturer Diesel, contacted GAAB and offered to take the photos. Flattered, Boblbee gladly accepted.

The result was a trendsetting, futuristic and very "urban" brochure that won the company a Danish design award. It showed lots of skin, funky people, and left plenty of room for imagination. Blanking also wrote a poem that was printed on the inside cover.

Without much of a marketing strategy in place, the company decided to show its products and let the potential users drive the positioning strategy. ISPO in Munich in 1998 was Boblbee's first international appearance. The company wanted to make a lasting impression but, with tight budgets and little understanding of its strategic positioning, it had to be innovative in its booth design. Piping from Spotlight was used to create a frame on which to hang the backpacks. Freight pallets were recycled as tables on which Boblbee displayed its "urbanistic" marketing brochures. Boblbee packing boxes were cut up to make signs on which Blanking wrote key words or slogans. ISPO turned out to be a huge success not only in terms of marketing, but also for product development. During the fair many mountain guides examined the harness and gave Blanking tips on how it could be improved. The company received lots of media coverage during those few days in Munich. One German journalist wrote:

> The queue to get into Boblbee's booth stretched all the
> way to the main train station in downtown Munich.

The German TV channel RTL was in attendance at the fair and covered Boblbee extensively. Overall the response gave the GAAB team new energy and trust in their idea. It was clear they had the new generation backpack on their hands…if only they could figure out the way to market it!

CUSTOMER VALUE PROPOSITION

So far, GAAB had operated mostly as a product-driven organisation. The product had been created to solve one of the partners' own transportation problems, and his experience was deemed to apply to a significant number of people. But several questions remained unanswered: how large was that population? What segment should GAAB treat as the target group? Where and how could they reach it? What were the key buying criteria of that segment? What price would it be willing to pay for a technologically advanced backpack? Did it even care about technology or was it mostly a fashion statement? What was GAAB's value proposition – a fashion statement based on Nordic design, a practical transportation means with unique ergonomic properties, a technology statement for techno freaks, a protection statement for safety freaks, or all of the above? Without a clear understanding of what the product stood for in the market, it was difficult to develop an effective marketing strategy. The initial marketing brochure had taken the product toward the trendy, urban group, but was that really what the founders wanted, or was it simply chance? Was this the most potent market segment or even the easiest one to reach? What implications would this positioning have for the future of the company?

The Boblbee backpack was best described as highly functional and sturdy, but it was also extremely trendy and it could therefore be used by many different customer categories:

- People doing outdoor sports would find the backpack light and highly functional. It could withstand wet conditions and hence was perfect for skiing, hiking or sailing. The Impact Protection™ not only shielded the carrier but also safeguarded the backpack's contents. The ergonomics of the pack made it suitable for carrying heavy weights for long periods, as the Lumbar Support System™ distributed the weight evenly and did not place stress on the back or shoulders.

- Another potential customer group was businesspeople. The backpack had been developed to be able to carry sensitive equipment such as laptops, mobile phones, PDAs and MP3 players, and the functionality was excellent. As such, it was easy for people commuting to work by train, bike, scooter/motorbike or on foot to keep things organised.

- Students often had to use their bikes to get to school, at least in towns in Europe, and they therefore needed a functional bag for their gear, laptop and study material.

- There were also opportunities to expand the product range to professionals such as police, ski guides, alpine rescue teams or medical staff who needed mobility while still being able to carry valuable goods with them.

- There was also the possibility of targeting trendsetters, who wanted to be different and always first with the latest products.

Without a clear decision as to the positioning of the product, GAAB had postponed making precise marketing plans. Possibilities included engineering cheap advertising campaigns through PR (public relations) in various newspapers and magazines, sponsoring key influencers and developing product placement. Other options were to continue doing trade shows (which had proved successful in Munich), in-company displays and event sponsoring. Yet another possibility was to invest a bit more and to develop a more purposeful marketing campaign (print media, TV, radio, etc.) that would establish the brand in the market, and build brand awareness and identity. A final option was for GAAB to agree to sell through an established consumer brand, such as Nike, Reebok, Adidas or Oakley. This form of private label production would shield the company from having to get involved in complex marketing and distribution issues. It would also provide the instant recognition of a global brand. But the partners first needed to make a decision regarding the product positioning.

SALES CHANNELS

Backpacks could be sold through many different distribution channels and a product like Boblbee, with its strong functional features and revolutionary design, was suitable for most of them. First and foremost, the product could be sold through traditional retail channels, such as fashion stores, travel gear specialists, sports and leisure boutiques, and even computer/IT distributors. These stores were often part of larger groups that provided regional, national and sometimes global advertising coverage and visibility. From GAAB's standpoint, they could provide immediate credibility and sales reach. On the negative side, the multi-layered distribution system, with intermediate wholesalers and distributors, ate significantly into the profit margins. There was also little control over the final sales pitch and positioning once the product was in the store. A close variation on the first model was the use of branded channels and stores, such as Nike or Adidas stores, or some other fashionable travel brands such as Timberlake. Selling the product under their brand names provided better recognition, but Boblbee would never be visible as a brand, just as a product concept, and being at the mercy of such retail behemoths did not provide much negotiation leeway.

A more radical option was to focus directly on corporate channels, selling the backpacks strictly through VIP promotions and sophisticated corporate gift specialists. These were often more directly connected to the clientele, hence reducing the total sales costs. But most corporate gift companies were relatively small without much brand appeal, and corporate PR opportunities remained limited. Since the backpack was originally designed with superior functional attributes (ergonomics, shock and water resistance, favourable aerodynamics, etc.), it was also possible to target professional users directly, or companies supplying professional workwear and accessories.

The alternatives did not stop there. Large malls were appearing in suburban areas, combining the offerings of dozens of smaller stores in a single convenient location. It seemed feasible to rely on Blanking's design skills to create a trendy in-mall store, based on an extended version of the display used at ISPO in Munich. This would shift the burden of creating hundreds of boutiques onto the company, and the partners were not sure that this was where they wanted to go. A recent trend in large department stores was the creation of stores-within-a-store, where a company was able to sell its products under its own label within the confines (and benefiting from the infrastructure) of a larger store. This was particularly appealing because it could help build Boblbee into a distinct brand while keeping the costs under control.

THE FOUNDERS AND EMPLOYEES

Patrik Bernstein was born in 1956. He is the president and CEO of GAAB. After a short career as a steward for Deutsche Lufthansa, he acquired a degree from the European Business School (at International University Schloss Reichartshausen in Germany) and started a career as an account executive at the advertising agency J. Walter Thompson in Frankfurt. After two years, he left the company to become a brand manager for Hasbro, one of the largest toy manufacturers in the world, in Nuremberg. In 1988 Bernstein was headhunted to Unilever Germany. After a few years in Indonesia, Bernstein returned to Germany in 1992 as general manager of Rimmel-Chicogo International, then a division of Unilever.

Sam Bonnier, born in 1959, is the chairman of the GAAB board. He is a member of the Bonnier family in Sweden, a large publishing house (Bonnier Group) with an annual turnover of €2.5 billion. Bonnier obtained a degree from the University of Denver and spent his first professional years in various companies in the Bonnier Group. In 1988 he switched careers and started selling equity funds for Alfred Berg Fond. In 1991 he started his own company, Office Complete Sweden AB.

Jonas Blanking is the youngest of the three (born 1966). He graduated from the Art Centre College of Design in Lausanne (Switzerland), before spending three years at the IDEA Institute in Italy. In 1992 he was appointed senior designer at Barré Design in Lyons and Paris, where he worked with Salomon (the sports equipment manufacturer). He later moved to Kontrapunkt Design in Copenhagen, where he worked with LEGO and Danish. In 1994 Blanking became a freelancer with his own studio in Malmö.

The Industry Environment

Boblbee competes within the apparel industry/sporting goods equipment market. In 1996 the global apparel and sporting goods market generated annual retail revenues of €130 billion (€85 billion wholesale) and was expected to grow by about 23 per cent by 2001. The US accounts for 50 per cent of all sales, followed by Japan, which accounts for 16 per cent (see Appendix 5C). The apparel industry/sporting goods equipment market is truly global and highly competitive, with a vast number of players. Sales growth is influenced by overall economic cycles, consumer attitudes and spending inclinations, and replacement of existing products. Other drivers for the sports apparel industry are the growing acceptance of informality (business casual) and greater health consciousness. Analysts expect that rapidly rising costs would put pressure on profit margins and consolidation would follow as a result. The global backpack market (a segment within the apparel industry/sporting goods equipment market) is large and it keeps on growing. It is difficult to quantify exactly how many backpacks are sold each year, but GAAB believe the number is into the millions. In Sweden alone, one of the largest sports chains sells over 100,000 backpacks per year.

Competition

GAAB identified a few potential competitors for Boblbee depending on the segment in which it chose to position itself (refer to Appendix 5D for a visual mapping of competitors). Some of the competitors are described in more detail below.

- Pelican: Pelican make technically advanced bags that target pro-fessionals. The bags are especially developed for cameras, mobile phones and laptops. Prices range from €70 to €300.
- MacCase: the bags were first produced for Apple Mac laptops, hence the name MacCase. The product range has been expanded to include backpacks, mailbags and briefcases. MacCase focuses mainly on the business community, but the bags are still innova-tive, trendy and colourful (think iMacs). They are also affordable and cost €30 to €80.
- Nike: over the years Nike has moved to become one of the most innovative sporting goods companies, always at the forefront of design. The company is a world leader in sports shoes, clothes and various sporting gear. At the end of the 1990s it began integrating

semi-rigid panels into its bags. Nike sports bags and backpacks cost between €50 and €200.

- Oakley: Oakley is positioned as the trendsetter in sporting goods accessories. It became world famous for its sunglasses and ski goggles, but later produced a wide range of backpacks, laptop bags, duffel bags, luggage bags and golf bags. Prices range from €50 for a simple mailbag to €250 for a wheeled travel bag. Most of Oakley's backpacks cost around €120.
- Salomon: unexpected and innovative sporting equipment and apparel are the hallmarks of Salomon. The company has started to move toward more technical clothes and also produces a wide variety of bags from duffel bags to boot bags, backpacks and various smaller bags. Prices range from €50 to €200.
- Arcteryx: the company is innovative in the material and technology used to produce its technically advanced bags. Arcteryx target climbers and skiers in particular, but also produce two bags with special laptop pockets for city dwellers. The price of an Arcteryx bag ranges from €100 to €500.
- EastPak: bags from this company are high quality "street packs". Their designs are traditional, but the colours follow fashion trends. EastPak has a wide variety of bags, including backpacks, totes, duffel bags, smaller travel bags and doggy bags, and lots of accessories such as wallets and mobile phone pockets. Prices range from €20 to €150, depending on the size and type of bag. EastPak has a no-questions product guarantee of thirty years.
- Hagflöfs: a Swedish manufacturer of outdoor gear, Haglöfs produces everything from backpacks – for climbing, skiing, long journeys and city use – to sleeping bags, clothes, shoes, tents and more. The company is famous for its high quality, long-lasting goods. Prices for Hagflöfs range from €44 to €275.
- Timbuk2: founded in 1989 in San Francisco, California, Timbuk2 targets students and young professionals, offering mailbags as a trendy alternative to backpacks and black briefcases. Later it extended its product line to backpacks, laptop bags, totes, duffel bags and handbags. The bags are colourful and highly functional. It is also possible to build one's own bag at the company's website. The bags range from €50 to €120 in price, depending on size and functionality.
- Ortovox: the company was founded in 1976 in Germany. At first Ortovox focused on producing measuring equipment and industrial automation systems. In 1985 backpacks were added to

the product line and in 1989 the company also started producing outdoor sports gear. Ortovox produce sports wear, backpacks and safety systems for outdoor use (mainly alpine). The products are of high quality and the company claim to be the number one choice of the pros.

- Samsonite: the travel luggage segment was Samsonite's focus. In the 1990s the company started to work with designers and became more fashion oriented, producing a wide variety of bags that are both functional and trendy. The intelligently engineered, practical bags are famous for their quality. The product portfolio also includes backpacks and mailbags, especially for laptops. The laptop bags are sturdy, highly functional and very durable, but rather dull looking. A Samsonite bag costs from €100 to €600. The company has also started to produce clothes and shoes especially aimed at travellers.
- Travelpro: Travelpro targets business people on the go and focuses on travel and computer bags. The company is innovative in its materials and functionality, but the designs are a bit dull, usually coming in black or other dark traditional colours. The bags can only be purchased in the US.
- Tumi: American Tumi focuses on design excellence, functional superiority and technical innovation. The product line ranges from travel bags, duffel bags and laptop bags to backpacks and mailbags for urban use. Tumi produces special mailbags with a modern edge for people who want a functional bag, but also one that is a bit more casual and exciting than a traditional business bag. Tumi's target market is professionals, but the bags vary from very traditional laptop and travel bags to more funky bags in order to accommodate the broad spectrum of business professionals. Tumi bags cost from €100 for the simplest laptop bag to €900 for a wheeled garment travel bag. Tumi also make stylish and lightweight bags (costing around €150).
- Eagle Creek: the company offers a wide variety of bags from wheeled travel bags, duffel bags, laptop bags, backpacks (they even have a special line called "parent survival pack") and shoulder bags to totes and accessories. Eagle Creek targets family-oriented professionals. The bags are very functional, but a bit boring in terms of colour and design. Prices for Eagle Creek products range from around €20 to €100.
- Delsey: founded in 1911 in France, Delsey initially made cases for typewriters, cameras and record players. In 1965 the company

started a department producing moulded plastic items that led to the introduction of hard-shelled suitcases in 1970. At the end of the 1990s Delsey was one of the leading luggage producers in the world. It is present in over 105 countries in five continents, with 6,000 points of sale. The company's product range includes two- and four-wheeled hard travel bags, backpacks, duffle bags, attachés and travel accessories. Prices range from €80 to €300. Delsey also has a wide range of backpacks: standard, urban and laptop, business ones with lots of compartments, as well as expandable and foldable ones.

- Other: many designer labels also make travel bags, laptop bags and backpacks. Prices start at €500, depending on style, size and label. Louis Vuitton, Gucci and Longchamp are a few of the designer labels active in the bag market. Companies such as Benetton also produce bags.

NEXT STEPS

Bernstein, Bonnier and Blanking sat in the hotel room and discussed the next steps for Boblbee. They had been so focused on delivering their backpacks to The Stadium and getting organised for the fair that they had no time to think about the future. Since the response at the fair was so enthusiastic, they needed to come up with a credible growth strategy quickly (i.e. a clear definition of the "valued customer", a distinct value proposition and all the elements of marketing, sales, distribution and production strategies). This was a pretty tall order for an evening in a hotel. On the hotel notepad, quick numbers jotted down seemed to imply that GAAB could possibly sell 15,000 Boblbee backpacks during the first year of operation (1998/1999), and that sales could grow annually by 15,000 units for the next three years. But estimating the sales was really difficult without a clear decision as to the key elements of the company's strategy. A great positive was that the existing suppliers were understanding about GAAB's situation and had promised a great deal of flexibility and responsiveness to its needs. This was important as some of the bigger stores (such as Intersport and Karstadt Sport) had lead times of up to one season, while smaller stores had greater flexibility.

With total sales so far of only 200 backpacks (in just two colours – black and silver – even though extra colours had been tested for the ISPO fair), the founders decided to focus only on the Megalopolis model for the rest of 1998, but to expand the product line in 1999 to include the People's Burden and the Box Jellyfish. These products share many of the innovations of the original Boblbee model, such as the harness system which would be identical for all three – a combination of black and dark grey in high quality Cordura. However, the bags would differ in colour, material and surface treatment of the hard shell and its various components, with Megalopolis being the most high-scale. Bernstein said, "at least we knew what our costs were and that helped a bit". For the Megalopolis model, the cost of goods sold is €36.74, for the Box Jellyfish it is €34.50, and for the People's Burden it is €32.89. The difficult question was where they should price the product. This would be impacted by the distribution and production structure they selected, which in turn would be picked to match the strategic positioning of Boblbee (refer to Appendix 5E for financial statements and projections for 1998/1999).

All in all, there was no way to escape the reality of the situation. They had a potential killer product in their hands, but unless they quickly defined its target clientele and an integrative marketing strategy, Boblbee would go where too many innovations had gone before – the product graveyard. The partners were not about to let that happen before they had given it all they could, and it would start that night.

NOTES

[1]This case was prepared by Professors Benoit Leleux and Joachim Schwass of the International Institute for Management Development, Lausanne, Switzerland, with the assistance of Research Associate Anna Lindblom. It serves as a basis for class discussion rather than to illustrate either effective or ineffective handling of a business situation.

Appendix 5A: **Spotlight**

Spotlight is a mobile, easy-to-build theatre stage. The stage is packed in an easy-to-carry bag and comes with classroom-ready acting sets – i.e. a teaching kit with scripts that had been narrated on CD (by a famous Swedish TV profile) with sound effects and music. There is also information about the play and the roles and some backdrops, as well as a guide for the teacher on how to get started. Some backdrops are printed to suit the plays; others are blank so the children could draw their own. Bernstein's idea is that Spotlight would be a way for children to learn through the arts and increase their self-confidence by getting positive and constructive attention. It would also allow them to improve their speech and communication skills. But most of all, it would allow children to have fun. The idea is also that the children would have to become involved in building the scenery and colouring the backgrounds. At the beginning of 1996 GAAB started market research in Sweden, which was used as a test market. The research, which consisted mainly of in-depth interviews, group discussions and actual performances, was carried out among children, teachers, childcare personnel, publishers and others involved in theatre and performing arts. The response was overwhelmingly positive. In the first year Spotlight sold 900 stages in Sweden.

Appendix 5B: **Capital Structure of Global Act AB**

January 1998

Source	Sum in Swedish Krona (SEK) (1 SEK = €0.11)
Founders' equity	300,000
Conditional equity	300,000
Short-term loans	1,178,000
Line of credit with Sparbanken Gripen	6,000,000
Loan from ALMI	500,000

End of 1998

Source	Sum in Swedish Krona (SEK) (1 SEK = €0.11)
Founders' equity	500,000
Conditional equity	750,000
Short-term loans	778,000
Line of credit with Sparbanken Gripen	6,000,000
Loan from ALMI	500,000
Other loans	1,500,000

Appendix 5C: **Global Sporting Goods Retail Market**

Worldwide Sporting Goods Retail Market, 1996

Total Market: US $130 billion

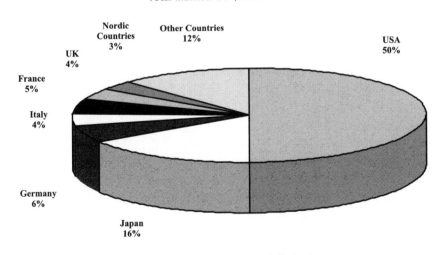

Source: Industry, Morgan Stanley Dean Witter Research Estimates

Appendix 5D: **Strategic Mapping of Competitors**

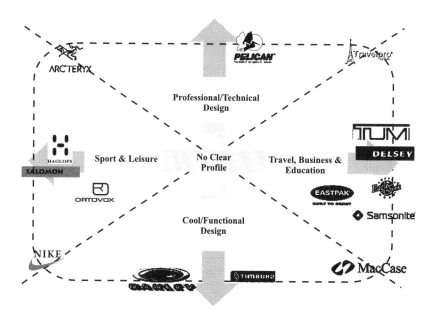

Boblbee

Appendix 5E: **GAAB Financial Statements**

Balance Sheet	1995/1996	1996/1997	Estimate 1997/1998
Assets	*(SEK 000s) (1 SEK = €0.11)*	*(SEK 000s) (1 SEK = €0.11)*	*(SEK 000s) (1SEK= €0.11)*
Cash	107	365	1,108
Accounts receivable	–	296	1,900
Other receivables	140	265	199
Inventory (Spotlight)	–	2,358	1,746
Spotlight in progress	321	91	96
Boblbee in progress	–	–	220
Inventory (other)	31	172	139
Activated plays	–	1,200	933
Total Assets	**599**	**4,747**	**6,341**
	1995/1996	**1996/1997**	**Estimate 1997/1998**
Liabilities & Equity	*(SEK 000s) (1 SEK = €0.11)*	*(SEK 000s) (1 SEK = €0.11)*	*(SEK 000s) (1SEK= €0.11)*
Share capital	300	300	300
Conditional share contributions	10	24	-1,402
Shareholder loan	–	1,371	778
Bank loan	–	3,713	5,900
ALMI loan	–	500	500
Others	–	–	400
Short-term loans	294	98	238
Accounts payable	279	166	874
Earnings	-284	-1,425	-1,247
Total Liabilities & Equity	**599**	**4,747**	**6,341**

News Aggregator Online

CHRISTIAN SERAROLS AND JOSÉ MARÍA VECIANA[1]

Marc Torres, co-founder and CEO of News Aggregator Online, S.L. (NAO), was sitting in his office on the evening of 22 June 2005 following a hard working day. He was not only tired but also worried. In the afternoon he had another long and heated discussion with his colleague Carles Blanch about the future of the company, particularly about the business concept and the growth strategy. The discussions with Carles had been frequent during the last months and the disagreement on the basic questions had become stronger. Marc and Carles had been working quite well during the first years of NAO but now the deep disagreement about the future of the company worried him greatly.

Marc felt that he was at a crossroads. On the one hand, he was happy and much satisfied to have been successful in starting a high-tech company that had created a powerful technology. After having developed products and solved financial problems, the company now stood on the edge of the growth stage. However, the different viewpoints regarding the future of the company had led him to consider actually leaving the company and going back to university. This would be a tough decision but one that Marc would have to give serious consideration to if an agreement with Carles on the future growth strategy could not be reached. Instinctively Marc began to review the start-up process of NAO, the problems they had had and the development of his relations with Carles. Perhaps the present situation is the result of some errors of the past, he thought, and he did not want to make another wrong decision.

SETTING THE BACKGROUND

News Aggregator Online, S.L. was founded in Girona, Spain in June 2000 by a group of young university graduates in the field of industrial engineering. In the meantime, the company developed an advanced system for tracking, classifying, managing and distributing digital information, combining the most innovative technology with journalistic experience. In fact, NAO is an intermediary operating in the online news industry, also called a web content aggregator (WCA). NAO delivers aggregated content to distributors and gives control to the subscriber. All of its services are subscription-based and targeted at the business-to-business (B2B) sector. In exceptional cases, NAO has also licensed its technology for certain applications. For example, in 2003 NAO licensed its technology to a provider of government and institutional information and gazettes. At that time, this provider used to have a large amount of personnel (documentalists and journalists) that did not provide any added value. Very early in the morning they would read, select and distribute information from those gazettes to CEOs, legal consultants and managers. The licensed technology developed by NAO was able to ease this process, making it more efficient and substituting this huge amount of personnel.

TECHNOLOGY, PRODUCTS AND SERVICES DEVELOPED BY NAO

Technology
The functioning of NAO's technology can be summarised into four different steps: 1) search/track and capture, 2) categorisation/index, 3) customise and manage, and 4) integration (see Figure 6.1).

Figure 6.1: **The Four Main Steps in NAO's Technology**

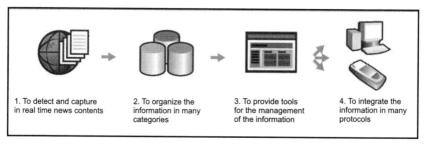

| 1. To detect and capture in real time news contents | 2. To organize the information in many categories | 3. To provide tools for the management of the information | 4. To integrate the information in many protocols |

Firstly, NAO's robots track relevant real-time information from an expansive list of publications in real time. An editorial staff carefully analyses and ranks each source for content quality and depth. New sources are continually added and refined based upon client requests and the changing online information landscape. In some cases, NAO also tracks images related to the news and even broadcast video and radio channels. Next, powerful filters enable businesses to tailor feeds based not only on the type of source but also content. Feeds can be built and filtered using keywords, Boolean logic and any combination of several descriptive metadata fields, such as category, author, language, SIC (Standard Industry Classification) industry codes, stock ticker symbols and even geographic location.

Once the information is categorised, NAO offers a management interface to customise all available options with the service: edit, delete or introduce keywords, languages, sources of information, type of content, etc. NAO also provides an interface to select the design of news feeds, to save information into different folders, to set up news alerts and bulletins, and to search for historical information, among other facilities. Finally, NAO provides a full list of integration options, including JavaScript, XML, RSS and more. Generally, an easy-to-use JavaScript wizard delivers precise control over the look and feel of the feed and then delivers JavaScript code that can be simply pasted into an intranet or website.

Products and Services

In the beginning, NAO focused on offering aggregated content into customers' applications such as websites, intranets, enterprise portals and emails. Until November 2002 NAO had marketed four services named PackBásico, PackPlus, PackSilver and PackGold. All these services are targeted to meet the needs of those websites trying to avoid the so-called "empty portal syndrome" (lack of updated content in their pages). In November 2002 NAO introduced press-clipping services to its portfolio. The triggering event to this line of new services was an order that came from a very important player in the sector, Presscut. Therefore, in January 2003, the services offered by NAO were divided into two lines: press-clippings and website content.

After NAO's first round of investment in the summer of 2003, a new business plan was prepared and new services were offered. To the two existing lines of services a new one was added: Technological Solutions. This new line of services was aimed at taking advantage of NAO's technology by applying it to meet the different needs of a firm. For example, a firm that had its own content but lacked a platform to efficiently classify and deliver this content to its employees, clients or providers would acquire a license for NAO's platform. Another example of the new target market was a firm that needed a search engine to search the large amount of data in its intranet. Currently, as of May 2005, NAO offers three main services: press-clippings, web content feeds and customised solutions. Table 6.1 summarises the main characteristics of these services. NAO contributes to the creation of value by reducing the information searching costs and aggregating the offer. Customers can access news headlines, full-text articles, company data and other content from several providers just dealing with NAO, lowering the number of interactions needed to conduct transactions.

Table 6.1: **Services from January 2003 to May 2005**

	Press-clipping	**Web Content**	**Technological Solutions**
Number of topics	1 custom	1 custom	
Keywords	10	5	
Access to news feeds' database	Yes (3 months)	Yes (1 month)	Newsletters, blogs, search engines, market analysis, repositories, platforms, etc.
Folders	50	–	
Mailing lists	3,000 mails	–	
Format	XML and HTML	XML, HTML, JavaScript, WAP, Flash	
Delivery	Email	FTP, HTTP, JavaScript	
Options	Up to 25 additional modules*	Up to 20 additional modules*	
Price	€60/month	€60/month	Depending on the service

*These modules offer added facilities like folders to store news feeds, real-time alerts, additional keywords, and access to repositories of news feeds.

THE FOUNDING TEAM

Although the founding team was composed of seven people, only three of them have worked in the business. Carles Blanch, who can be considered the "inventor", was twenty-five years old when the firm was founded in June 2000. Although he was finishing his master's degree in industrial engineering at the University of Girona, he had always been interested in computers and programming. At the age of twelve his parents bought him a computer, a Spectrum, and he started to self-learn programming. When someone asked him why he had chosen industrial engineering instead of computer science he answered that you did not need to study computer science to be able to program applications, you learn it by doing. He argued that what is really important when one needs to program something is to understand fully the phenomenon, and therefore a good and broad university study like the one provided by industrial engineering is the best.

Carles comes from a family that has always been very entrepreneurial. His father, after working for several years in the plastic industry, created a factory that produces roll-ons and plastic packages for the cosmetic industry. When Carles was only nineteen he created his first new firm with his uncle's help. It was a helpdesk for users who were not familiar with computers, providing telephone assistance for a monthly fee. He was the only worker and his uncle provided the funding. However, after six months the business was not very successful and it ceased its operations. Later, while studying his master's degree, Carles began to work part-time for a website-developing company in Barcelona. Some months later, he was invited to become a partner in the cooperative, so he left his studies and moved to Barcelona. His adventure lasted almost three years, the time that it took him to realise that his objectives were really different from his counterparts, so he quit and went back to the university in Girona where he met Marc.

Marc Torres, a 25-year-old industrial engineer, can be considered the "promoter" or lead entrepreneur of NAO. In 1999 he had joined the European Doctoral Programme in Entrepreneurship and Small Business Management, a Ph.D. programme organised jointly by the Autonomous University of Barcelona and Växjö University, Sweden. At the University of Girona he was both teaching and working on his doctoral dissertation about "success factors of dotcom firms" when he met Carles. Actually, it was not the first time that they had met because they both had started their master's degree in industrial engineering in 1993. However, each of them had his own circle of friends, although their families knew each other and they had several friends in common.

Marc had always been a bright student, being the first in his class both in high school and in his master's degree. During his doctoral studies he became interested in creating a new venture in the Internet, although he had no personal business experience. His father and mother were both university professors, though his father had his own engineering consultancy business dealing with construction projects. Marc's grandfather on his mother's side had a very well known jewellery shop in Girona, dating from 1834. On his father's side, the family had a successful butcher's shop. Although Marc's business experience was limited, he had frequently helped his grandfather at the jewellery shop, and when he got his degree he worked with his father in the engineering consultancy business. At university Marc was teaching a postgraduate course in electronic commerce and several summer courses. The director of his department offered him the chance to set up a new subject: electronic commerce. Thus, he organised the full new course from scratch. These activities provided him with an outstanding knowledge and contacts in this particular field. Hence, University of Girona was the first university in Catalonia to have a postgraduate course on electronic commerce, an embryonic subject in Spain in 1999.

Finally, Robert Llach was the last co-founder who also worked in the company. He was one of Marc's best friends and graduated in accountancy. Marc and Carles were looking for someone who had practical experience in accounting and administration, someone reliable and willing to face new challenges. Therefore, Robert was their best option. Robert was also twenty-five years old at the founding of the firm and since he was eighteen he had worked in several companies (real estate agents, construction companies, banks, etc.).

The founding team was completed with four more people in order to complement the team's competences and capabilities. Marcel and Roger were contacted to join the project. They had both created a marketing consultancy company a few years before. Their company was very successful and they founded a second company, a marketing research firm. Moreover, they were thinking of expanding their businesses and the Internet was a very attractive sector for them because they wanted to build an online consumer panel to conduct marketing research.

Marcel was from Girona. He had attended the same secondary school as Carles and had gone out with Carles' eldest sister. He was thirty-one years old and had a master's degree from the University of Barcelona in marketing research and a bachelor's degree in international management and commerce from Portsmouth University. Before establishing his marketing consultancy company he had worked as a technical expert in market research at Hewlett Packard and PRM International, where he met his future business partner. Marcel was also a part-time lecturer at Barcelona University in the Faculty of Economics and Business. Furthermore, Marcel's father had his own business, a consulting firm in Girona with over thirty workers. Roger, a 33-year-old graduate from the Barcelona University holding a master's degree in business administration, had worked as a product manager in Henkel Ibérica and PRM International before establishing the firm with Marcel. He was also a part-time lecturer at Barcelona University in the Faculty of Economics and Business.

David (thirty-five) and Josep (thirty), both of them journalists and quite bohemian, were the last to join the team. Like Marcel and Roger, they also had parallel careers. Firstly, they both had studied journalism at the Autonomous University of Barcelona. Secondly, they also had broad experience in the press and in the television sector. Finally, they were working together for the 3xl portal, the official portal of the Catalan regional television station. They were the owners of Postpop.com, the musical portal that Carles developed while he was working in the website developing company in Barcelona, and the first to have the idea to create a robot to integrate news stories from other music portals into theirs. Thus, they were really happy to be involved in the project although they would not work on it.

ORIGINS AND DEVELOPMENT OF NAO

At the end of 1999 Marc was working as assistant professor at University of Girona, doing research in the field of electronic commerce and ebusiness when he came across an old university peer, Carles. At that time, Carles was still finishing his master's degree and working part-time as a free-lancer developing websites. Marc was a member of the Catalan Industrial Engineering Association (COEIC) and helped them in IT (information technology) matters. The COEIC wanted to change its information system and develop a website to provide services to its associates. As Marc was in charge of the project, he proposed Carles to build up COEIC's new web-site. In December 1999, when the website was almost completed, Carles showed Marc a very interesting project he had been implementing in his previous job. It was a music magazine's website that after six months of operations had ran out of money and the owners could not afford new articles. These owners (David and Josep), who were well-known journal-ists, asked Carles to create a robot (an advanced software system) to track, capture and classify news from other music portals and to integrate them into their music magazine's website. This robot would search the main music portals in the Internet for news and articles related to music events. Then, it would classify and integrate those news items and articles into the main page of their music magazine. This technology avoided the so-called "empty portal syndrome" by providing a continuous flow of updated feeds to that website.

Carles was very surprised to see the success of this technology in that website. Not only did the number of visitors not decrease, but it began to grow steadily. Marc showed a great interest in this technology because it could be a very promising business opportunity. Therefore he asked Carles to create a new firm with him to exploit this concept. The opportunity that Marc saw was to expand the use of this searching technology to any website that looked for information, not only related to music. In fact, the idea was to generate an online news aggregation platform to cover the informational needs of any website. In addition, this platform could also be used for competitive intelligence purposes. This was the embryo to what later became the first content aggregation venture in Spain.

Before Marc and Carles took the decision to create the new firm to exploit the opportunity, they started to investigate the market and looked for similar initiatives in Spain and in other countries. They found a start-up, called Moreover, created in August 1998 by Nick Denton, an ex-*Financial Times* journalist who was able to obtain investment from Atlas Venture and a group of Amazon.com executives in June 1999. Moreover defined itself as the leading online news aggregation service in the world. Its sophisticated harvesting technology aggregated news and information from over 1,500 web sources in near real-time, and then assembled web feeds into more than 300 categories. Later in June 2000, Moreover was able to raise $21 million from Reuters. Marc and Carles were very excited to discover a new company that was already doing what they were planning to do and that had been able to obtain funds. On the spur of the moment they both decided to go with the idea of creating a firm. Their main motivation to create a new firm was the challenge to invent and exploit something new that did not exist at the moment. They were also tired of working for others and wanted to develop their own project.

PLANNING STAGE

The founding team invested a tremendous amount of effort initially to determine the needs of different potential customers for the services they were planning to offer. This phase lasted approximately five months, from January to May 2000, and followed four main steps: definition of the business idea, extensive competitors and market analysis, complementing the founding team, and preparation of the business plan and investment proposal.

Definition of the Business Idea

First of all, Marc and Carles wrote down the business idea they had in mind. The following paragraph is the transcript of Marc's answer to what the business idea was:

The idea was to develop a content aggregation platform to gather, categorise and deliver online news. We wanted to offer it to websites that couldn't afford real-time, reliable and relevant online news. We also thought that we could offer a free news portal to end users, where they could easily monitor any information that they wanted. For example, if you're a Madonna fan, you could define an email alert to receive daily any information related to her in your email account. Our initial idea of a revenue model was advertising because in early 2000, advertising was the most important source of income for most Internet-based firms. Advertisers were paying between €30 and €200 per every thousand pages that users visit, so the key point was to have a lot of traffic in your site. Just imagine that you have 1,000,000 viewed pages per month, which makes €1.2 million per year!

Based on their definition of the business idea, they investigated the main needs that such a service was required to meet. According to Marc, they wanted to provide a service that covered the following needs:

- Track relevant real-time information from an expansive list of publications, including premium international and regional news sites, corporate websites, government press pages, weblogs, discussion boards, and more.
- Classify this information into pre-built topics or custom topics for rapid delivery of precisely targeted news.
- Provide tools to efficiently manage all of this information: search facilities, email alerts, format options, etc.
- Deliver and integrate all of this information into custom applications: websites, intranets, enterprise portals, emails, etc.

The main benefit of this technology is the time and costs savings on the localisation, classification, delivery and integration of online precisely targeted news. Therefore, NAO could provide online press clipping services, integration of news feeds in portals and database news searches among other services.

Extensive Competitors and Market Analysis
The next step that the founders took was to roughly analyse the market, basically in two directions: (1) was there any company offering similar or substitute services in Spain, and (2) what were the main characteristics

that made this service useful for users? Their approach to these questions took different forms. Firstly, they looked for similar initiatives all over the world. The result was a very accurate comparative table between the different competitors in this market, including those selling substitute products. All of this information was based on a content analysis of their websites. The variables analysed in each case were date of founding, brief description of the firm, technology (proprietary vs. non-proprietary, indexing, categorisation, customisation, delivery, etc.), content (number of sources, online vs. offline, news, articles, papers, business information, etc.), services portfolio (characteristics, prices, promotion, etc.), clients, sales volume, financial ratios and founders.

Following this gathering of information, they roughly analysed the demand side by focusing on consumer studies of what users appreciated the most in a website, and how websites obtain real-time information to update the content on their webpages. According to Marc:

> All of the studies that we reviewed showed that Internet users generally look for updated online news, with at least 30 per cent of them having access to online newspapers. Besides, websites have understood that updated content helps to retain buyers, so many of them are beginning to demand aggregated content for their websites.

All of the information gathered in this step helped the cyber-entrepreneurs to detect a gap in the market and to gain knowledge of the sector they were planning to enter. Marc and Carles also stressed the difficulty in finding information about competitor and customer needs due to the novelty of this service. One of the main barriers they detected was the unwillingness of both websites and users to pay for content; everything was supposed to be free at that time in the Internet.

Complementing the Founding Team

After defining their business idea and understanding how the market worked, Marc and Carles realised that they had to involve more partners to successfully develop their project because their main competences were in technology at that moment. They needed partners with marketing, financial and journalistic backgrounds and experience. In fact, according to Marc, there were three main pillars in that project that needed to be considered: technology, content and marketing. While the entrepreneurs started to write down their business plan, they also began to look for partners to complement the team. Therefore, they first contacted Robert, who was very experienced in finances, as previously mentioned. With this initial team, they informally presented the project to a marketing consultancy business that was owned by friends of Carles – Marcel and Roger. They immediately showed a great interest in the project because they thought that it could help to build up a consumer panel among the users of the news portal to conduct market studies on consumer preferences. Furthermore, they were able to involve the owners of the music magazine's website that had initially proposed to create a robot for content aggregation purposes. With these new partners, the content, the technology and the marketing pillars were established. Interestingly, it took a short time to complement the team.

Preparation of the Business Plan and an Investment Proposal

The process of preparing the business plan was complex, interactive and time-consuming. At the beginning of April 2000 Marc and Carles had already written down their first business plan draft that was presented to the founding team. The plan included an investment proposal and the distribution of the different tasks and shares among all the team members. This last part was probably the toughest to negotiate. According to Carles:

> We all agreed on almost every aspect of the plan, but we really had a difficult negotiation regarding the distribution of the shares. The main problem was that some of the members of the team would not join the project to work in the company, they would only provide equity, others would work part-time, while others would work full-time. Finally, some would just provide temporary work. So, you can imagine the difficulty in trying to reach an agreement on the percentage of equity of each team member.

After a month of discussions, they came to an agreement and decided to share out the equity according to the contribution to the company (i.e. work and money provided by each partner). Taking a time frame of three years, they calculated the total budget of the project. Then, they computed the contribution of each partner in terms of money and labour, thus resulting in the distribution of shares in the following percentages: Carles 25 per cent, Marc 24 per cent, Robert 5 per cent, Marcel and Roger 14 per cent each, and David and Josep 9 per cent each. At the beginning, Carles, Marc and Robert would not contribute any money to the equity because they provided labour without being paid by the company. This was the agreement reached with the rest of the founding team. They would work for a year without wages but after this time they would begin to earn a wage according to their responsibilities and capabilities. Should NAO not be able to pay such a wage, their accumulated earnings would be considered as a contribution to the equity and the total equity would be increased proportionally.

At this point, the end of April 2000, the team started to review the business plan draft and after four brainstorming sessions the first business plan was finished. However, they all agreed that a more accurate market analysis was needed to successfully define their products and implement the business idea. Marcel and Roger offered themselves to develop an offline market research study to identify the target audience, whether the market for it was big enough, and on what conditions future customers would buy the services. According to Carles, a mistake was made at this stage that later provoked problems between Carles and Roger, and between the working vs. non-working founding members of the team:

> The team did not talk about who was going to pay for this study; we just did it. Later on, Marcel and Roger requested the money their company spent on such research but I did not agree on the quantity. In fact, I think it was a sort of revenge for the wage policy that we approved.

IMPLEMENTATION STAGE

The implementation stage lasted from June 2000 until the end of November 2001, when a redefinition of the business was accomplished. Marc went to different public administrations to find out what support was available for the creation of a new firm and obtained legal advice at Girona's town council free of charge. This help implied that NAO could be given vouchers that could be used to pay consultants, lawyers and agencies helping the team in the administrative task of legally constituting the firm and writing the formal business plan. The next step was to register the name of the firm and the trademark at the central registry office. A lawyer wrote down the company's bylaws. The company was officially constituted on 29 June 2000 by the public notary. The process of legally constituting the firm had taken two months and had cost approximately €1,750. According to Marc, there was too much bureaucracy in this whole process:

> It was incredible the number of forms that we had to fill in and the time that it took to constitute the firm. We could hardly believe that we spent two months in the process

and paid almost €2,000 to have nothing at all, except the right to begin our operations.

While they were legally establishing the firm, they also found a 60 m² cheap office in the centre of Girona and rented it.

WORKING TEAM

From the beginning, only Marc, Carles and Robert were working in NAO. The rest of the members of the founding team did not work in NAO, although they took part in the meetings of the board of directors, and coordinated and developed certain tasks apart from providing money. For example, David and Josep were in charge of the content; they selected and classified all of the sources and coordinated the tasks of the documentalists. They also defined all of the processes needed to successfully maintain the database and the different categories and key words needed to classify the information. In addition, they helped to define the rules that the robots should follow to obtain and classify the information. Marcel and Roger were mainly the capitalists and the marketing advisors. They provided the initial equity to create the firm (approximately €36,000) and they also conducted the market analysis. Unfortunately, they failed to provide contacts from their network of customers to whom the services of NAO could be sold.

Three more people were involved at this stage and they were selected according to the tasks described in the business plan. First, a software engineer helped to develop the first platform and he was later hired by Nokia. Second, a database services technician configured the internal network, servers and other systems, like databases. Third, a documentalist was in charge of the news sources database. Both the software engineer and the database services manager were recruited at the university where Marc was teaching. They were still finishing their degrees and they both needed to do an internship in a company, so it was quite easy to involve them in the project at a very low cost.

Initially, NAO was very similar to a garage start-up. The funding was just enough to develop the first platform but everyone knew that more funding would be needed in the near future. According to Carles:

> Our initial idea was to demonstrate that we could do what we had planned. It was risky, a challenge, but we were convinced of our capabilities. Furthermore, our business plan was structured in two phases: the prototype phase

where the main objective was to develop the platform without the need for big investments, and the launching phase where we would need much more investment and support to make the business grow.

PRODUCT DEVELOPMENT

Before having the capability to develop the platform, the founding team had to spend two months setting up the office and buying servers, furniture and other necessities. This was a tough job but all agreed that it helped to integrate and build the team spirit of the working founders. According to Robert:

> I still remember polishing the floor, painting the walls, fixing the electrical wire, etc. I would never do that again, it was really hard; the next time I'll pay for it. However, it really helped to get to know each other; we were all in the same boat.

Finally, in September 2000, everything was ready and the working team started to develop the technology. For five months, the team worked very hard to develop the first news aggregation platform in Spain and launched NAO's website in the first week of February 2001. During this period, Carles focused on the technical problems and on coordinating the development team consisting of three members. Marc also helped in this task, but he mainly focused on commercial issues. He visited many potential customers to show them the developments with the platform and to gather suggestions that would help to improve the service. He also compiled marketing databases and websites in which to advertise their service, and also scanned the environment for new competitors, trends and opportunities. In summary, Marc focused on every aspect related to the marketing plan, although his experience was not in marketing. David and Josep also gave some support in this task, but less than expected. Robert mainly focused on administrative and financing matters, but also helped Marc in his commercial task.

The Internet bubble of the late 1990s was remarkable by almost any measure. In 1999, 294 Internet firms went public, raising more than $20 billion. By 1 March 2000 Internet firms had a combined market value of $1.7 trillion, reflecting a spectacular rise in stock prices: between January 1999 and February 2000 the Internet Stock Index (ISDEX) more than tripled in value. Perhaps more impressive, however, was the subsequent fall in valuations. By the end of 2000, the ISDEX had returned to its level on 1 January 1999. It fell another 69 per cent over the subsequent nine months, for a total decline of nearly 90 per cent. Such a price drop was associated with the arrival of adverse news that triggered a significant change in investor expectations. This change in the environment significantly affected NAO. Marc and Carles realised that the business opportunity that they were planning to exploit would not provide enough revenue to survive. Therefore, they organised a meeting with the rest of the founding team to redefine their business model. This change of orientation was conducted in two parts. The first redefinition took place while they were still developing their services and technology in this implementation stage, while the second redefinition would take place after the first sales were made.

FIRST REDEFINITION AND PRODUCT LAUNCHING

Regarding the first redefinition phase, they changed their initial plan of offering a free news portal to end users because advertising fees were exponentially declining, so they could not expect enough earnings from this revenue model. Therefore, they focused on providing content to websites, intranets and extranets. Based on subscriptions, websites would pay a monthly fee for a continuous flow of aggregated content to their websites. Interestingly, NAO had already an order before the launch. This order came from one of the visits that Marc performed in the previous stage and it became a sort of beta-tester for NAO's services. The next step was to decide what marketing actions were needed while taking account of their lack of budget for any marketing campaigns. Considering that all of their customers had a website (a compulsory requirement for the service), the team decided that the best channel to promote their services was the Internet. According to Marc:

> It is really difficult when you don't have much money to carry out marketing actions; you have to struggle with your brain to come up with a wise idea to cheaply advertise your services. In our case, this was an affiliate network, a webmasters' network to test our technology free of charge. It was a real success, within a month we already had over 2,000 affiliates.

They thought that the best way to promote their services was to offer them free of charge. However, they had to think about a solution that would quickly penetrate the market and, at the same time, did not cannibalise their own professional services. Therefore, they studied several web services available on the Internet such as free email. The idea was to offer an affiliate programme consisting of some pre-selected topics that a webmaster could easily integrate into their own website with its own design in a couple of minutes. These pre-selected topics had an advert with the sentence, "do you need free headlines in your web?" that invited other webmasters to sign up for this affiliate service. This initiative was very successful and at the end of 2001 NAO had reached over 17,000 affiliates. This database of potential customers was NAO's first source of orders. Moreover, it helped to build NAO's brand and awareness in their sector.

GETTING FINANCE

Thanks to the awareness obtained through the affiliate initiative, NAO successfully participated in many contests related to business plans and technology firms. During this phase, they also applied for financial funding to two important programmes and got them. The first one was a programme called Technological Trampoline, which provided almost €90,000 in funding to develop advanced technology in content aggregation. This programme was offered by the regional government (Generalitat de Catalunya) to those technology-based companies created by university researchers and professors. The second one was a programme called Neotec, which provided a €200,000 soft loan (the loan had only to be repaid if the company succeeded in commercialising its services) and it also was to be used to develop advanced technology in content aggregation. This programme was offered by the national government to those new prospective high-growth technology-based companies. Marc and Carles spent almost one year doing all of the paperwork and preparing the application for these programmes. The financial funding given by these programmes was tied to the condition of an increase of the equity by the same amount (i.e. €200,000). In order to carry out this equity increase, the team focused on negotiating NAO's first round of investment with Ericsson and Retevisión, the sponsors of the e-entrepreneurship contest organised by the regional government that NAO had won in July 2001. These sponsors had the obligation to invest 50 per cent of the funding needed by NAO, up to €300,000, if the company provided the remaining 50 per cent, which was already obtained through the above two programmes.

Unfortunately, these sponsors did not fulfil their obligation due to the critical financial situation that Ericsson and Retevisión were facing during 2002. As Marc highlighted:

We did spend a lot of time negotiating with the sponsors, we accepted all of their requirements because we thought that it could launch NAO but they did not act in a fair way. We had even done two due diligences, one technological and one financial. They were obliged to invest in NAO according to the contest stipulations but they didn't. In November 2002 we decided to take legal action against them for breaking the rules.[2]

At this point, NAO's financial situation was very delicate because although it was significantly increasing its sales, its expenses still exceeded the revenue so that the company was running out of cash (€84,658 in sales but €103,469 in operating costs at the end of 2002). Secondly, wages were very low, far below the market. The working founders were seeking an increase of their wages from the non-working founders. Finally, the company could not obtain the funds that they had won in the programmes and contest because the team did not have enough money to increase the equity by €200,000 to comply with the conditions. The deadline for increasing the equity to obtain the programmes' funds was June 2003.

This whole situation created serious problems among the founding team members, especially between the working and non-working founders. The situation almost led to the closure of the company. Carles and Roger had so many big arguments on the issue that they have not talked again to each other since then. Carles was demanding an increase in equity to pay decent wages, even though the increase would not be sufficient to comply with the conditions of the contest. But Roger considered that the team should go on with the effort of earning low wages until break-even was reached. The rest of the team mediated in the dispute and proposed an intermediate solution that led to a sufficient increase of the equity to be able to raise their wages.

Fortunately, in November 2002 a very big purchasing order came from the biggest traditional press-clipping company in Spain, Presscut. This company wanted to integrate NAO's services into its platform and they had heard about NAO when it participated in a business plan contest. This order and a subsequent increase of the equity by €60,000 proportionally provided by all of the shareholders in January 2003 was a ray of light in the darkness. In addition, NAO began to capitalise on the marketing actions implemented in this stage. In parallel, NAO contacted a regional governmental business angels programme called ARC, which had the aim of putting new companies in contact with private investors. This programme worked pretty well and within a month a contact was established with two business angels (Efund and Newsfund) who were very interested in NAO, with negotiations starting in January 2003. In fact, the process was very quick because NAO had already conducted all of the due diligences needed for the funding process when negotiating with Ericsson and Retevisión. Therefore, in June 2003 NAO closed its first round of investment. The business angels provided €140,000 of funding and received 22.5 per cent of the equity. With this increase of equity, NAO could get the €90,000 and the €200,000 from the above-mentioned programmes. A board of directors composed of Marc, Carles and a member of each of the two business angels was constituted. The distribution of shares before and after this first round of investment is shown in Table 6.2.

Table 6.2: **Distribution of Shares Before and After NAO's First Round of Investment**

	Before investment round (June 2003)		After investment round (June 2003)		
	%	Equity	%	Equity	Surplus
Carles	25	24,015.18	19.375	24,015.44	0
Marc	24	23,054.58	18.6	23,054.82	0
Robert	14	13,448.50	10.85	13,448.65	0
Marcel	14	13,448.50	10.85	13,448.65	0
Roger	9	8,645.47	6.975	8,645.56	0
David	9	8,645.47	6.975	8,645.56	0
Josep	5	4,803.04	3.875	4,803.09	0
Efund	0	0	15	18,592.60	74,887.17
Newsfund	0	0	7.5	9,296.30	37,443.58
Total	100	96,060.74	100	123,950.67	112,330.75

Efund was formed in 1989 and was actively involved in Eastern European countries. Newsfund was formed in 2003, coinciding with the investment in NAO. It was a young investment company specialising in new technology projects. It was expected that Newsfund would contribute to NAO, besides money, with its technological know-how and its experience in marketing of services related to ICTs (information communications technology). Together with the constitution of this new board of directors, the by-laws were changed. Among others, the following decisions had to be approved now by the Board with three favourable votes: increase of equity, the annual budget, the signature of contracts over €10,000 and an increase of wages over the cost of living. The result was that the two new investors, with only 22.5 per cent of the equity, controlled the company. In the beginning Marc and Carles were excited about the new board because they thought that it would help a lot, especially in the marketing of NAO's services. However, after some months, they both realised that the new directors were not contributing as expected. Most of the board meetings were used to explain to the investors what the company was doing. Marc and Carles also realised that they would have to make the decisions by themselves. In addition, the bureaucratic work increased because Marc had to prepare a report for the board every month.

Practically all of the money from this investing round was devoted to marketing actions. A sales manager (Albert Vila) was contracted and a new office in Girona was rented. Two software engineers and an administrative person were also employed. At this time, Robert was helping the sales manager and Marc, although he was the CEO, also helped in selling. NAO assigned 10 per cent of the budget for marketing campaigns. The result was significant and at the end of 2003 NAO was already selling €212,149, more than doubling its revenues from the previous year.

SECOND REDEFINITION

The order that came from Presscut in November 2002 and the frequent meetings held to coordinate the integration of aggregated content into Presscut's network of websites drew the attention of Marc and Carles to a new service that many of Presscut's clients were demanding: online press-clipping services. This fact led to a second redefinition phase of NAO's business model. NAO's founding team realised that their technology could be applied to offer a service that they had not thought of at the beginning: press-clipping services to documentary departments. In Spain, this sector was worth over €60 million in sales per year. In addition, Presscut had over 20 per cent of this market, TNS another 20 per cent and the rest of the market was very fragmented. The team saw a very interesting opportunity to diversify its business and began to adapt its technology to offer all of the applications required to effectively provide such a service. Within five months, 25 per cent of NAO's sales came from this new online press-clipping service. In May 2003, NAO had already reached the monthly break-even and it also received a first bid from Presscut to buy a part of its equity. For this company, NAO had already become a strategic issue.

FUTURE BUSINESS CONCEPT AND GROWTH STRATEGY

Albert Vila, the new sales manager, who was selected jointly by Carles and Marc, reported to Marc. Since his incorporation into the company, Marc and Carles began to have arguments on how to manage growth. For example, Carles thought that Marc's supervision was too close while Marc thought that Albert was not capable of managing the sales department of three people. Marc thought that Albert was a good salesman and very committed to NAO but did not know how to lead a team. In order not to quarrel with Carles, in May 2004 Marc decided to reduce his monitoring task and his sales activities, and allowed Albert more freedom, including assigning him a sales budget. In the summer of 2004, the sales manager proposed to open a new office in Barcelona and to hire three salespeople. Marc asked Albert for a budget but he was unable to prepare it alone and requested Marc's help in this matter. They both prepared the budget based on Albert's forecasts and it was then approved by the board of directors. At this time, the relationships between Carles and Marc had become worse and even a psychologist was contracted to help reconciliation.

In December 2004, the Barcelona office costs were further exceeding its revenues. Sales forecasts had been too optimistic and actual sales were 25 per cent behind Albert's forecast. Most of Albert's marketing actions had not succeeded and he did not even realise that some of his salesmen were doing a poor job. For example, one of salespeople did not sell a single service within six months. Moreover, the sales team argued that Albert spent a lot of time selling but fully neglected to coordinate and coach the sales force. He was unable to organise the selling activities in a systematic way and neglected to control the results of sales force. In addition, new competitors from abroad were appearing on the scene. For example, Google and Yahoo developed GoogleNews and YahooNews, which in certain cases could substitute NAO's services. Therefore, this provoked a new reorganisation. The major actions taken were:

- The Barcelona office was shut down and two salepeople were fired. The sales manager and a salesperson were incorporated into the Girona office. Additionally, the sales manager had to report the sales force results to the board of directors and he could not spend a single penny without Marc's approval.
- A big effort was put into NAO's ERP (enterprise resource planning). This ERP was developed inside the company due to the uniqueness of the services commercialised by NAO and the fact that no single ERP's existing solution in the market would satisfy its requirements. At this point, NAO's development team focused

on implementing a CRM (customer relationship management) system to take control of the offers and customers. They wanted to know the conversion rates they had, the time it took a potential customer to buy the service, the costs associated with a sale, the costs of a campaign, etc. Marc also had to define a new sales system and the data that the salespeople would have to introduce in this ERP to successfully control offers and sales.

- Brainstorming sessions were conducted among all the members of the team (fifteen people at that time) in order to think about short-term actions that could provide cash to the company. These sessions led to the development of new services, such as repositories, CDs to store all of the information generated by a client in a year and new potential clients.
- Carles began to delegate his technical management tasks and focused on commercial issues. He tried to start a new line of services: technological solutions. In fact, he looked for additional applications of the aggregation technology already developed by NAO.
- Some of the budget items were cut, for example communication costs (€1,700 per month).

All of these actions began to produce some results in May 2005, when NAO had nearly reached its break-even point again (see Table 6.3).

In the meantime, the relationship between Carles and Marc had worsened. Besides the different viewpoints on the marketing strategy, there was a deep disagreement between them on the future business concept and growth strategy. Marc thought that NAO's core competence was the development of technology related to aggregation purposes and that their biggest weakness was selling. Moreover, the cost of obtaining a new client was too high to maintain a large sales force (each contract, worth an average €720, required €240 in client direct commercial costs). Therefore a different marketing strategy was needed. Marc's idea was to franchise its technology to press-clipping companies that would sell these services. There was also a second acquisition offer made by Presscut that would guarantee NAO's survival and would enable them to apply its technology to other press-clipping services (audio, TV, etc.). Furthermore, big Internet groups like Yahoo, Google and VeriSign began to be interested in this sector by developing aggregation technology and acquiring companies. Meanwhile, Carles wanted to be completely independent from any other firm, and maintain or even enlarge the marketing department. Hence, their main disagreement was in the very different alternatives: whether NAO

Table 6.3: **Information from the Profit and Loss Account and Balance Sheet**

	2002 (€)	2003 (€)	2004 (€)	Jan– May 2005 (€)	May 2005 only (€)
Sales	84,658	212,149	277,848	155,826	38,705
Operating costs	103,469	251,446	350,021	188,745	39,704
Profit	-18,811	-39,297	-72,173	-32,919	-999

should in the future be a technological or a service company. Apart from this basic disagreement, the psychologist also identified a big difference in Carles' and Marc's leadership styles and the way in which they handle daily operations. This difference led to a division of the whole team into two subgroups: one in favour of Marc and the other in favour of Carles. The question was – would this arrangement work?

NOTES

[1] This case was prepared by Christian Serarols and José María Veciana of the Universitat Autònoma de Barcelona. It has been prepared as a basis for class discussion rather than to illustrate either the effective or ineffective handing of an administrative situation. Name of the company and all names are disguised.

[2] The case is now at the Supreme Court of Catalonia and the decision is not expected before 2008.

Appendix 6A: **Terms and Definitions**

B2B: is the exchange of products, services or information between businesses rather than between businesses and consumers. Although early interest centred on the growth of retailing on the Internet, forecasts are that B2B revenue will far exceed business-to-consumers (B2C) revenue in the near future.

CRM: short for Customer Relationship Management. CRM entails all aspects of interaction a company has with its customer, whether it is sales or service related.

ERP: short for Enterprise Resource Planning, a business management system that integrates all facets of the business, including planning, manufacturing, sales and marketing.

JavaScript: is a programming language developed by Netscape to enable Web authors to design interactive sites. JavaScript can interact with HTML source code, enabling Web authors to spice up their sites with dynamic content. JavaScript is endorsed by a number of software companies and is an open language that anyone can use without purchasing a license.

RSS (Really Simple Syndication): is a document type that lists updates of websites or blogs available for syndication. These RSS documents (also known as "feeds") may be read using aggregators. RSS feeds may show headlines only or both headlines and summaries.

Web Content Aggregator: is an entity that can transparently collect and analyse information from multiple web data sources.

Weblog: a diary-style site, in which the author (a "blogger") links to other web pages he or she finds interesting using entries posted in reverse chronological order. A weblog is similar to a diary or journal that is organised, managed and made available through a website.

XML: Short for Extensible Mark-up Language, a specification developed by the W3C (World Wide Web Consortium). XML is a pared-down version of SGML, designed especially for Web documents. It allows designers to create their own customised tags, enabling the definition, transmission, validation and interpretation of data between applications and between organisations.

Academic Work

KENT THORÉN[1]

In April 2001 two exchange students were having a vigorous discussion in a small café on Plaza Mayor, Madrid. The two young entrepreneurs, Jeremias Andersson and Patrik Mellin, were close friends, even though they had met for the first time only a few months previously at a Stockholm University student banquet. Their discussion, this sunny afternoon in Madrid, resulted in the conception of what would eventually become a very successful enterprise. Over the months that followed they continued to develop their idea until Jeremias, Patrik and Jeremias' old friend Johan Skarborg founded Academic Work later that summer. The goal of the company was to exploit the deregulated employment market in Sweden, by taking an intermediary role helping companies to get in contact with students for part-time assignments. Initially, they ran the business as a sideline to their university studies, and the first "student consultants" were friends and friends of friends. Patrik managed the business in Linköping in parallel with his studies in human resource management and work science. Johan was studying law in Uppsala and initiated the business there, while Jeremias started the business in Ronneby, as he was a student at Blekinge Institute of Technology.

The business model utilised by Academic Work was quite simple. It primarily involved offering students' help with assignments such as simpler IT (information technology) consulting, building a webpage or designing a database. Academic Work, acting as the recruiter and formal employer, invoiced the customers based on students' time reports and then paid the students their salary after deducting a margin. Practical details and the daily activities were agreed between the client and the students directly. The company slogan "Rent a Student" described the service in an accurate and concise way, and it soon became evident that there was a strong demand for student consultants. The firm expanded quickly, and by early 2002 Academic Work was established in four cities. At each of these locations they rented a small office and staffed it with one or two students who managed local activities on a part-time basis. These students were called "project managers".

Today, Academic Work is Sweden's leading temporary help agency specialising in employing university students. Turnover has increased annually and the company generates a healthy profit. Nevertheless, the path to today's prosperous operations has been neither easy nor straight-forward, as the entrepreneurs had to deal with turmoil, changes and many challenges along the way. In order to achieve the business expansion and manage its consequences organisational participants have adjusted their way of working and the firm's internal practices on several occasions.

THE EARLY DEVELOPMENT OF THE FIRM

By late 2002 Academic Work had established activities in the four major university cities in Sweden: Linköping, Lund, Uppsala and Stockholm. Based on the market response (each office quickly secured a few accounts), there appeared to be a strong possibility of making a little profit for the year – as long as costs were under control. The consultants worked on an hourly basis, which was directly connected to the revenue that they created, so there were no practical limits to the amount of temporary help the firm could deliver as long as the administration was handled effectively. However, attaining profit from the cash flow required constant attention to the number of permanent employees hired, which meant that organisational growth had to be well paced.

During those early days the project managers had to do a wide range of tasks including interviewing students, marketing Academic Work on campuses, scouting for prospective clients, dealing with contracts, selling, matching students to projects, following up on projects, and reporting to Head Office. At the same time, most of the project managers also had their own schoolwork to maintain. Running operations in this form, with loosely committed part-time project managers, eventually turned out to be highly problematic. In particular, project managers seemed to have difficulties handling the scope of their broad role. As a result, most of them tended to prioritise some of their tasks at the expense of others. Jeremias explains:

> We had worked for a year... with other students who were doing this on a commission basis on the side of their schoolwork. They thought it was fun to meet other students and to go out and sell this. But we noticed that running activities with students as project managers...

was... incredibly difficult – because personnel turnover was high, and they required much training and delivered little. So we felt that we needed more continuity.

However, inspired by the initial success the three entrepreneurs felt that the business idea had good potential, but in order to take the venture to the next level changes were needed. Firstly, the founders managed to raise about €64,500 in seed money from savings and FFF sources[2] so that they could hire a few full-time employees to staff the offices properly. Secondly, they decided to establish some formality in the basic operations so that the firm would progress from the individual unorganised efforts of the start-up phase towards a more purposeful and focused set of activities. Hence, they defined a few roles (i.e. two or three) with a more limited set of responsibilities than the previous project management role. The assumption was that better-defined roles would enable employees to focus on a smaller set of activities that matched their interests and competences more closely. At the same time, it was expected that this change would improve performance through the benefits of specialisation.

Assignment 1

Your first assignment is to help Academic Work to organise for this stage of their development in order to **achieve business growth.** In particular:

- Consider the activities needed to operate the business. Try to group the tasks and define a small number of roles to which these groups (or sub-sets) of tasks can be assigned [hint: design your business process or business model as a starting point].

- Use the results from above to make an organisational chart.

- As the entrepreneurs put more of their own and other people's money at stake, they felt a need to improve control of the business to ensure that business growth was systematically pursued by everyone. Propose how to control each role and also the student consultants.[3] Describe for each role a short set of controls in adequate detail. Base your proposals on what should be the desired behaviour from individuals in each role. Keep recommendations realistic and effective given the situation. You can make reasonable assumptions regarding constraints, etc.

BUILDING THE BUSINESS

The success continued! Role specialisation led to a significant efficiency boost – which continued to improve as the formalisation of tasks, routines and methods progressed. The definition of roles initiated a gradual transition towards a departmental structure that has prevailed since it was fully implemented in 2003. At the end of 2002, the founders managed to raise some venture capital with the help of an experienced industrial manager called Anders Jonsson, who also agreed to become the chairman of the board. With €650,000 in venture capital (paid out in portions over 2003 with the achievement of agreed firm-level goals), it was time to go full throttle with the business, and hire and train a number of new employees. In early 2003 the firm had twelve people employed, but the exact number varied greatly over time because personnel turnover was still quite high as a result of internal changes and new demands put on employees. With surging confidence and better financial strength, the vision was to "roll out quickly" and establish offices in all thirty-three Swedish cities with a university or college of higher learning. But these dreams were to be revised and a more realistic plan was worked out together with Anders and a representative from the venture capital firm. Gradually, decisions were made to prioritise Linköping, Göteborg, Lund (that office later moved to Malmö), Stockholm and Uppsala. The rest of the branches were liquidated over time. In addition, two of the founders (Johan and Jeremias) moved to the office in Stockholm, which became the firm's headquarters. About a year later, Patrik moved to Stockholm as well.

As a result of experimentation and client requests it was natural to broaden the range of temporary help services. It made economic sense to provide basically whatever help the client wanted, within reasonable and legal limits, as long as there were students willing to accept the assignments. In late 2003, Academic Work had clients in a wide range of industries, but the bulk of the revenue came from large volume assignments at call centres, warehouses and supermarkets. However, there were always some students engaged in missions demanding competences that were more "academic", like market research projects, IT consulting and different types of investigations.

Business growth was driven by a very strong, explicit and nearly obsessive emphasis on sales. This was also reflected in the company culture. For example, sales were normally the first point on the agenda on all internal meetings. The sales force was noticeably result-oriented with a strong competitive spirit. One of the salesmen described his first impressions when joining Academic Work:

> ...it was a Friday when we had a booking competition [i.e. booking sales meetings]. Everybody was booking meetings! At other companies the attitude can be, "it is impossible to book meetings on Friday afternoons" and other such excuses... here people work hard!... Among the sales organisation that I have worked for, none has been this hard working.

The venture capitalists had a very benevolent and hands-off attitude towards the management of Academic Work. Still, external ownership and an experienced manager on the board made the founders realise that they could no longer freely run the firm exactly as they wanted. Questions were suddenly asked about the firm's cost structure, performance and plans. Answering how many prospects there were in different segments, how many clients that had been approached, the number of proposals sent and the profitability of ongoing assignments was not something that was routinely done before. Formal goals and plans had to be produced and financial milestones had to be met. On the other hand, the entrepreneurs all concur that they benefited a lot from the advice and support they got, and that it was very useful to have mentors to rely on for ideas and input. During a board meeting in the second half of 2003, Patrik Mellin was given the responsibility to evaluate the control systems and to suggest how they could be changed in order to enhance growth further. The board requested explicit measures to drive and evaluate progress. But Anders pointed out that the strategy was not a pure top-line growth mission any more; bottom-line growth (profit) was becoming important as well. He explained how this is a natural step once the business idea had proven its sustainability and seemed to be possible to grow with:

> Today, we deliver a couple of hundred thousand man-hours so the margins are important. A few crowns per hour make a difference. Therefore, we needed to put more focus on the assignment administration and cash flow, as profitability was increasing in priority.[4]

Moreover, in case of problems, quality measurements were initiated as the larger amounts of money at stake made managers increasingly concerned with customer satisfaction and quality. When asked if a large customer complaint occurred as an antecedent of this shift in awareness, one employee answered:

No, it was no particular event.... It was in August [2003] really that we realised, we had hired people and grown very fast and we had to start paying attention to the mistakes we were making – so it didn't go too far. It was then, maybe a year ago, that we realised how important the large clients are... we wanted to look at "what do our twenty largest customers mean for our turnover?" for example. "What mistakes are we doing out there?" as we need to fix them. The fear of losing such a large client has led to the quality awareness.

These perceived risks and defensive motives implied that quality control was a response to consequences of business growth since the founders only took action to protect their revenue streams after they were attained. When the business was small there was little at stake to worry about. However, as sales increased managerial participants became conscious of how much money the business really involved and grew more anxious about potential failures. This meant that the awareness of consequences of potential failure increased as business has grown. In addition, some larger clients had formal quality requirements for procurement of temporary help. The first action then was to reduce the lack of insight into these issues, by starting to measure complaints and gather statistics. Patrik's proposal (see Appendix 7B) attempted to take all of these considerations into account.

REMAINING CHALLENGES

Academic Work achieved substantial business growth despite a declining market trend, which indicated that they had acquired a competitive advantage. By focusing on the part-time services market niche, Academic Work attained a cost advantage compared to the large competitors[5] who generally had to pay a 75 per cent guarantee salary, even when their consultants are not on assignment. Moreover, the customers seemed to appreciate having students complementing their own workforce, which provided a positive differentiation from the large competitors. Jeremias, now holding the sales manager role, explained:

Students are fast learners, they are ambitious, hardworking and motivated. Partly they are motivated to going out and getting some work experience, but also to make some money and build some personal contacts. So it is a rewarding group for us to work with.

104

More direct competition was provided by approximately fifteen other student temporary help companies.[6] Some of these had been in the market longer than Academic Work, but the latter had a small advantage in its broader range of services, offering students for any type of work, whereas several of the competitors offered only more qualified "education-related" assignments to their students.

During 2003, 2004 and 2005 the firm continued to grow both the business and the market share, thereby establishing and maintaining a leadership position in the segment. The managers seemed convinced that tighter growth-oriented controls and increasing formalisation of work contributed strongly to the excellent development of the business. The potential for further growth appeared to be very good because of the focus on a high-demand niche, combined with the leverage achievable from information technology (i.e. the use of Internet and databases for building and administrating the student stock on which the business is based). Anders made the following comment on the advantageous nature of the business:

> This business idea is well suited for growth because it is cash-flow intensive. Once a critical mass is reached, the cash needed for growth is generated by the business itself. And today, there is enough cash for handling potential problems and for financing growth. And there are no large step costs either [no large investments needed in production technology, etc. for further expansion] and volume can grow without much impact [on the organisation].

Interestingly, during 2005 the strategic situation changed in ways suggesting that the niche was getting more mature. Some of the larger competitors appeared to have noticed the profitability of temporary help using students and hence opened their own operations in this area, although still in a small scale. A more serious threat was Adecco's acquisition of Kulan, one of the student consultant competitors.

Academic Work has so far stayed true to its initial business model and focused on driving growth, without being distracted and dispersing efforts in the pursuit of other business opportunities. Inspired by the mentors, the philosophy has been to grow by exploiting the original business idea while continuously getting better and better at what they are already doing. However, for some time there has been some doubt about how long this approach should be maintained. Some of the entrepreneurs are starting to get nervous about the need for proactive steps to secure future cash flow before the current business model moves into a stage of decline. Because firm and product life cycle stages are normally only visible in retrospect, it might be a good idea to start new business development before it is too late – especially when the competition is changing.

Moreover, managers have felt a growing pressure to introduce more "professional management" practices in the firm as it keeps expanding. In particular, the organisational growth (i.e. people and units) accompanying business growth (i.e. top and bottom line) has triggered frequent challenges. A small group of three administrators was added to the organisation in the beginning of 2004. Their task is to handle invoicing, accounting, salary payments, etc. But there was a feeling that the general organisational expansion itself has been a source of turmoil, friction and even conflicts. Inspired by an article in the *Harvard Business Review* (see Churchill and Lewis, 1983[7]) that indicated a strong need for simultaneous handling of delegation and control issues within the firm's growth phase, Patrik suggested that it is time to attend to organisational problems more explicitly.

Patrik conducted a number of interviews to gather relevant information for dealing with the internal problems. It seems that the administrative department does help to ease the workload, but frustration amongst employees remains. In Stockholm, the situation appears better than at the (now) six local offices, but there are complaints that the founders are busier nowadays and usually not available when they are needed. Employees (of all roles) further claim that they could be more effective and develop their skills better if top managers were more involved. Both the managerial workload and the increasing complexity inside the firm appear to have grown much more than management has realised.

In previous years, the founders used to visit each office regularly. But as Patrik moved to Stockholm and everyone became more occupied local offices started to experience some problems as a result of the less frequent visits. In particular local offices feel poorly informed and less involved in the company, which tended to make their employees demotivated. Changes in the firm appear to be especially frustrating. Patrik discovered that because these employees were isolated from the discussions behind changes, they had little chance to influence decisions or even understand their purpose. Hence, local office employees often became more, rather than less, confused when receiving information from Stockholm. Even though a weekly newsletter had been introduced, it was not an effective solution to this problem. The critical issue appeared to be that the context of change and the interaction where ideas are formed are not transmittable without "rich" information channels. Instead, the "thin" text information in the newsletter often made local office employees confused to a much larger extent than the actual issues might justify, as it triggered anxious speculations about what was happening "over there" in Stockholm. This was reflected in several interviews, for example in the following conversation with an employee in Lund:

> We are not aware about new policies and similar things. We just go; "really, did we have that!? – 'Yes we had that for six months' – okay!" It is very confusing and we feel left out and forgotten.
>
> Like the dress-code, for example, that is claimed to be so important – "do we have a dress-code!?" It is enough that it happens once, really, to make you start to think about how much else you might be unaware of.
>
> But it is not only the changes. For example, there are also the large consultant assignments. It can be useful to know if we lose a large client, so you don't assume for a year that we work with someone when we don't. Stuff about clients, and what's happening in the company, who is employed or leaves, and structural changes and so on. If it happens a few times and you feel under-informed, you feel that you don't know what's happening – or that you don't know if you know what's happening.

Assignment 2

- Should Academic Work continue to focus on student temporary help or should they re-evaluate their strategy? What could be potential areas for future growth? [Hint: Use clear reasoning and specify both opportunities and threats.]

- Specify typical consequences of growth based on the case story and on other assumptions that you can justify.

- Draft your recommendations for changes to address the consequences of growth at Academic Work and for other adjustments that might be needed in order to make your recommendations work. Suggestions should follow from structured argumentation and solid reasoning.

NOTES

[1] This case was prepared by Kent Thorén of the Royal Institute of Technology, Stockholm. It has been prepared as a basis for class discussion rather than to illustrate either the effective or ineffective handing of an administrative situation.

[2] FFF – Family, Friends and Fools.

[3] E.g. *personal controls* like selection, training and culture; *diagnostic controls* like performance measurements and rewards; and *action controls* like rules, formal work procedures and policies. Alternatively, you can use the framework described by Simons, R. (1995) "Control in an Age of Empowerment", *Harvard Business Review*, March–April, pp. 80–88.

[4] Profitability has also had a positive trend over the years: -41.1% (2000), -4.4% (2001), 7.9% (2002) and 9.4% (2003).

[5] For example, Manpower, Proffice and Adecco.

[6] Such as Kulan, Skill, Studentkraft and Komet.

[7] Churchill, N.C. and Lewis, V.L. (1993) "The Five Stages of Small Business Growth", *Harvard Business Review*, May–June

Appendix 7A: **Business Processes: Overall Business Process (Academic Work)**

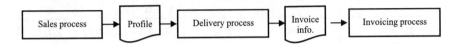

The account managers provide recruiters with a consultant profile, specifying the assignment's requirements when ending the sales process, and thereby starting the delivery process.

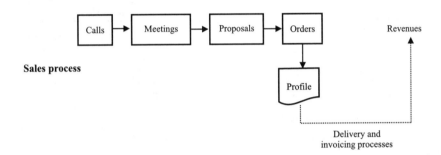

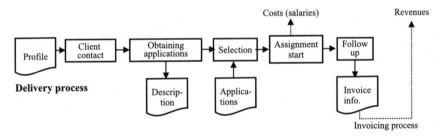

To verify and supplement the consultant profile, recruitment activities include a contact with the client company. A description of the assignment is posted on a job list that is available on Academic Work's website. Applications are then submitted through the Internet by students who have registered themselves in the database.

Appendix 7B: **Performance Management (Result Control) Systems at Academic Work**

Measurement	Span	Department*	Base Data	Targets	Reward
Sales, firm turnover	Collective	1 & 2	Output	Monthly	Conference destinations
Margin	Individual	1	Output	Monthly (and weekly)	Commission
Margin	Individual Collective	2	Output	Monthly	Commission
Sales (orders)	Individual	1	Output	Weekly	–
Sales calls	Individual	1	Effort	Weekly	–
Sales meetings	Individual	1	Effort	Weekly	–
Delivery (staffing assignments)	Individual	2	Output	Weekly	–
Customer contacts	Individual	2	Effort	Monthly	–
Student contacts	Individual	2	Effort	Monthly	–
Quality, customer complaints	–	2	Output	Monthly	–
Quality, lost orders	–	2	Output	Monthly	–
Quality, consultant complaints	–	2	Output	Monthly	–

* Department 1 and 2 refers to the actual structure at Academic Work, but the actual department names are hidden, since it is a part of assignment 1 to make your own independent proposal of a structure.

Appendix 7C: **Financial Information**

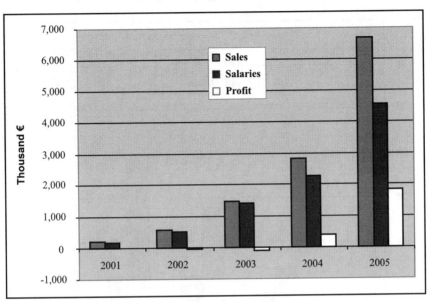

Financial progress overview chart. Salaries include both the students and the full-time employees. €1 = 9.3 SEK.

Appendix 7D: **Financial Data (Thousands €)**

Fiscal Year	Sales	Office Costs	Other Costs	Salaries	Profit
2001	204.3	17.2	0.0	186.1	1.0
2002	559.1	34.4	53.8	515.6	-44.7
2003	1,457.0	51.6	96.8	1,411.6	-103.0
2004	2,838.7	51.6	129.0	2,274.2	383.9
2005 (projection)	6,666.7	60.2	215.1	4,568.3	1,823.1

Appendix 7E: **Organisational Information**

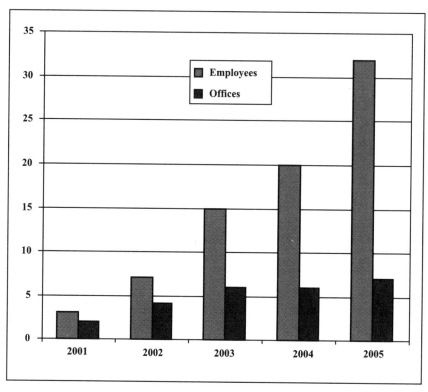

Number of employees including the founders (full-time equivalent) and the number of offices.

H&H Oy

JANE SILVER[1]

Harri and Hanna Pessa sat down at the farmhouse kitchen table. The guests had just finished breakfast and the various activities for the day were being led by the team of activity leaders. Harri and Hanna needed to discuss where they thought the future of their business was going, particularly in light of the recent changes in the pulp and paper industry in Finland. They had a number of issues to look at and so they cleared the kitchen table, got out a large piece of paper, and decided to draw a mind map of the business and its developments to date. They started with the family and its business activities.

THE PESSA FAMILY BUSINESS

For generations the Pessa family had owned forests in the Northern Region of Tampere. Finland is about 338,000 square kilometres in area, making it one of the largest countries in Europe. Forests cover three-quarters of the country's surface area and the other outstanding features of Finland's scenery are some 190,000 lakes and approximately as many islands. The Pessa family forests included seven lakes and crossed a number of valleys. For generations the family had tended the forest, felling trees for the local pulp and paper factories, as well as providing wood for furniture. The continual planting of trees to maintain the stock of wood was an ongoing process. Originally, before the large pulp and papermaking factories were built, the Pessa family (like many local foresters) had their own pulp-making capabilities. Over time it became uneconomical to produce their own pulp and their grandfather finally decided to concentrate on the felling and planting of trees that were sent to the larger pulp factories close to Tampere. When Harri and Hanna were young the machinery held a fascination for the twins; they could remember it being used and the smells and

113

sounds associated with the production of pulp. Their father, Timo Pessa, continued to develop the forests and also branched out into tourism.

The closest town to the Pessa forests is Virrat, which is a small town north of Tampere. It developed in support to the local forestry industry and more recently markets itself as a tourist destination. It has an open-air museum which shows how people lived and worked in the past, and which provides visitors with the opportunity to buy traditional handicrafts. A number of self-catering apartments are available for rent and in the summer a steamer arrives at Virrat Harbour following the Poets' Way trip from Tampere. The area around the town provides rugged countryside, lake vistas, ponds, streams, bubbling rapids and of course the deep, dark forests. This is an area that provides a wealth of leisure opportunities ranging from riding, rambling, canoeing and cycling to fishing, boating and, in the winter, sledging and skiing. Timo Pessa saw the opportunity to provide farmhouse accommodation for tourists, as well as building a number of log cabins on the lakesides that could be rented out both in winter and in summer. Visitors would come to stay in the lakeside cabins, rent his boats and fish in the lakes or go walking in the woods. The cabins were furnished to a very high standard with their own sauna and fully equipped kitchens (including microwaves and dishwashers). As the cabins became more popular, people began asking about which walks to go on in the forest. Timo decided that there was enough interest to provide guides who would walk with the visitors, pointing out the various stages of the forestry growth, as well as local fauna and flora. From this developed a whole series of activity guides, thus opening up the market to activity holidays for the whole family to learn new skills, whether it was boating, canoeing, fishing, rambling or skiing. The activity holidays were very popular and supplemented the income derived from the forests.

The twins Harri and Hanna Pessa were born in Virrat and attended the local schools. In their secondary school studies they paid a visit to the Serlachius Interactive Museum in Mänttä. The history of the paper industry in Finland is closely associated with the town of Mänttä and the Serlachius family. The museum traces the history of papermaking and the various processes that it goes through. It was the former headquarters of the Serlachius company to which the Pessa forests had provided wood and wood pulp. The decline of the industry (as in the case of the Pessa wood pulp manufacture) forced the company to close its operations. However the Serlachius family did not want the history of papermaking in the region to be lost and hence developed the factory into an interactive museum, as well as using some of the premises as an art gallery. Harri and Hanna were fascinated with the demonstrations and the actual hand-making paper activity. Upon their return home they went into the wood pulp sheds that housed the pulping equipment. The machinery, although old, was still in working order as it was used as part of the guided activity "From Wood to Paper". As the summer was approaching, the twins decided to add an additional feature to the From Wood to Paper guided tour. They would make some paper in the traditional handcrafted way.

TRADITIONAL PAPERMAKING

Ancient papermaking involved boiling the stems of plants or other suitable materials to loosen the fibres. The product was then mixed with water and poured through a sieve, dried, and from this came a raw sheet of paper. Finer meshes, pressing and drying developed papermaking into the craft of handmade paper of today. The development of the papermaking industry led to the use of wood pulp for papermaking. Wood pulp can be either ground (mechanical) pulp or chemical pulp, with both processes using co-niferous trees. To make ground wood pulp, the bark of the tree is removed in barking drums in which logs are tumbled against each other and against the sides of an open cylinder built of girders, under a constant spray of water. The bark-less trunks are then placed in tall magazines and pressed against a grindstone, which reduces them into fine fragments and bundles of fibre. These are washed through screens where the coarser material is removed by jets of water.

The moulds on which handmade paper is formed consists of rectan-gular wooden frames across which is stretched a fine wire gauze on which there is usually worked in brass wire a design, or initials of the firm or manufacturer of the paper. A narrow wooden frame called a deckle fits over the mould to form a frame for the gauze. The vat man holds the mould with the deckle attached, vertically dips it into the suspension of pulp, brings it to a horizontal position and, scooping up a little too much of the pulp mixture, raises it from the vat. Shaking the mould from left to right and back to front, he is able to spread the fibres evenly over the mould and obtain a close-knit rectangular sheet of paper equally strong in all parts. The deckle is then removed and the mould set aside and allowed to drain until the coucher turns over the mould onto a piece of felt and presses it carefully to transfer the sheet from the mould which is then removed for the vat man to use again. Interleaved piles of paper and felt are made to a height of 45 centimetres and are then pressed by a hydraulic press to squeeze out all the residual water. These are then dried in warm air. The paper sheets, if they are going to be used for writing paper are then sized in baths of gelatine solution and the final glazed appearance, for writing quality paper, is achieved by passing the sheets through zinc or copper plates and heavy rollers. When the paper is held up to the light the design that was worked in the brass wire shows through as a watermark.

PESSA HANDCRAFTED PAPER

The demonstrations of papermaking by Harri and Hanna were very successful. Adults and children alike were fascinated in watching the process from a tree to a sheet of paper with a watermark. The original watermark of *H&H* was worked in brass wire and as the pair became more adept at working with the brass wire, so the range of different initials and designs were demonstrated. The large paper sheets were cut down into writing paper size and then sold to visitors. Harri and Hanna worked on the different designs, textures and colours of the paper and produced a range of handcrafted products, such as watermarked papers, wrapping papers and cards. They began to populate the tourist and craft shops and attend craft fairs in the area with samples of their designs. Interest in the paper products was shown by a number of people (ranging from companies to craft shops, department stores and private individuals) who wanted to have their own watermarked paper. As the demand grew for the products, Harri and Hanna needed to employ more people to make the paper. The only parts of the process that modern mechanised applications were adopted were in the pressing of the papers and in order to dry the papers heated drying sheds were used. The crafted paper business grew from strength to strength locally and soon orders were coming in from places such as Helsinki. The twins decided that it was time to move some of the production to a more centralised location.

FINLAYSON COTTON MILL

The rural landscape of the Tampere region is characterised by waterways, forestry and farmlands. In contrast, the city of Tampere is a growth area for the location of companies. The redevelopment of the Finlayson-Tampella industrial area provides a unique opportunity for the location of companies. According to the Ministry of the Interior, Tampere has attained an indisputable number one position in Finnish regional centres. A corridor of development has been forged between the region and the capital Helsinki. The central core of the development is based on the former Finlayson cotton mills. This former cotton factory was established by Scotsman James Finlayson who came to Finland from St Petersburg in the early nineteenth century. By the beginning of the twentieth century Finlayson became the largest industrial company in the Nordic countries. Its final decline was in the 1970s as the pressures in the cotton industry became such that it could no longer compete with the growing industries in China and India. The factory is located right in the heart of Tampere city on the banks of the Tammerkoski rapids. The renewal of the area began in the 1990s and was finally complete in 2004. The 100,000 m^2 of space houses the Tampere Polytechnic School of Art and Media, and has been let to over 100 companies, attracting such diverse businesses as ICT (information communications technology) companies and media companies (as well as many firms from the creative fields). The area has a number of restaurants, cafés, and craft and gift shops.

PESSA HANDCRAFTED PAPER AT FINLAYSON COTTON MILL

The development of the cotton mill afforded Harri and Hanna the opportunity for which they were looking. They decided to increase the manufacturing of handcrafted paper by setting up design workshops and drying rooms in the Finlayson complex. The wood pulp would be brought down from the Pessa vats in Virrat by road. The workshops were open daily for guided tours. To compliment the tours, they opened a craft shop stocking the range of products that they produced, as well as taking orders for bespoke papers. Tampere was a fast growing city with many conferences and new businesses locating in the city, and the tour of handmade paper became a feature for many visiting business and conference delegates. Orders increased and craft shops and department stores in Helsinki not only sold the standard range of papers, but also started to take orders for the bespoke Pessa handcrafted papers. Orders were also coming in from the neighbouring countries of Sweden and Norway. These orders started slowly but soon there were regular orders being exported.

PULP AND PAPER INDUSTRY

Harri had read a report titled "Pulp and Paper: At the Crossroads" by Olli Manninen in *Finnair Bluewings* magazine (May 2007) that surveyed the challenges facing the pulp and paper business. Interviewed for the report were leaders of the almost €400 billion industry worldwide. One of the questions the report considered was why profitability in the sector had collapsed in recent years. The demand for paper worldwide had changed dramatically with almost half of all papermaking machines being sold to China as the demand for paper in Asia had exploded, with the Indian and Russian markets also showing rising demands. Conversely, the European and North American markets were no longer growing as the communications industry (which traditionally consumed a lot of paper) was quickly becoming electronic. In Europe, as manufacturing overcapacity increased real prices for paper slumped. Metsäliitto Group CEO Kari Jordan told the newspaper *Helsingin Sanomat* that prices were so low that manufacturers hardly earn anything from a roll of paper, even though their machines are constantly setting new production records (Metsäliitto Group is the world's tenth largest forest industry group). The report "At the Crossroads" went on to comment that the Finnish and international giants in the forest business were worried not only about the shift in demand for paper, and the consequential implications for pulp manufacturers, but also that know-how in the field was also moving away from Europe. This could also be seen in the lack of investment being put into product development in the pulp and paper sector.

FINNISH PULP AND PAPER INDUSTRY

Despite the dark clouds over the forest products market, Finnish experts expressed cautious optimism about the sector's ability to improve its competitiveness. Firms in the field were seeking cooperation to boost their competitiveness by creating highly refined products and customer solutions. The Finnish forest industry cluster aimed to double the value of its products and services by the year 2030 with plans to increase its investment by about 150 per cent with help from the state. The forestry industry is still a major employer in the country with an estimated 200,000 people from a total national workforce of just under two and a half million. However, in the future it is envisaged that the actual wood fibre will increasingly come from South America, while the actual markets will be concentrated in China and elsewhere in Asia.

THE PESSA FAMILY BUSINESS – THE MIND MAP

As they talked through the various factors, so the mind map of the business grew. Hanna recounted to Harri her recent visit to the Business School in Virrat, which is part of Pirkanmaa Polytechnic. They were running a European Union-funded intensive programme which involved undergraduate participants from eight European countries working together in groups to provide business solutions for pan-European working. Hanna had been asked to present the case study of the Pessa family activities, which the students were going to use as a basis for designing marketing and strategic plans. She had attended the session on "Working Across Cultures" which she found very interesting and had also made her reflect upon some of the traits she had seen in European visitors to the farm and cottages. Both Harri and Hanna had recently attended an international conference for small businesses that had been held in Turku. They found it interesting to meet not only academics and other entrepreneurs, but also to attend some of the practical workshops. The mind map was complete and now the conclusions from the various sections needed to be drawn and action plans put in place for the business. As a starting point they decided to set the business in the context of the country:

Finland

Finland is a Nordic country with neighbouring countries Sweden, Norway and Russia, as well as Estonia on the other side of Gulf of Finland. The growth rate of Finnish GDP has been approximately 3 per cent in the last few years. Services industries constitute 66 per cent of the Finnish GDP, secondary production (industry) 31 per cent, and primary production (agriculture) 3 per cent. There are three important export sectors in the Finnish economy: electrical and optical equipment account for about 25 per cent of exports; metal products, machinery and transport equipment account for about 30 per cent; and wood and paper products account for about 25 per cent. The fourth biggest export sector is the chemical industry. Finland has around 5.3 million inhabitants. Almost two-thirds of them live in urban areas and one-third in rural areas. Approximately one million people live in the capital area consisting of Helsinki and its neighbouring towns. Principal cities are Helsinki (population 561,000), Espoo (232,000), Tampere (204,000), Vantaa (187,000), Turku (175,000) and Oulu (129,000). Virrat is to the north of Tampere and is part of the Tampere Region.

Farmhouse Accommodation and Log Cabin Rental

Hanna looked at the booking spreadsheets for the last three years. Her conclusions were that the bookings for these were consistent throughout the year. There were ten staff employed who covered the catering and servicing in the farmhouse and acted as activity guides. The activity holidays were particularly popular with more requests for accommodation than could be provided. This area of activity, coupled with the guided tours of the story of papermaking, provided sufficient income to pay the salaries of the staff, refurbish accommodation, cover the running costs of the farmhouse and still make a profit. There was sufficient capital retained from this set of activities to consider building some more log cabins.

Forestry

The maintenance of the forest was a year-long process with felling and planting planned for each of the strands of trees. Each area had its own ten-year plan and the team of twelve (drivers, fellers and planters) were busy all year long. However, Harri felt that this was an area, given the state of the global and national industry, which could present problems in the future unless other markets could be developed for the timber.

Pessa Handcrafted Paper at Finlayson Cotton Mill

This was a success story. Originally starting with one vat man, a coucher and three people to supervise the drying, cutting and packaging of the paper, the compliment of staff had risen to three vat men, three couchers and eight people working between the drying, printing and packaging areas. Two full-time guides were employed to take parties of visitors around the factory and explain the processes, with the tour ending in the gift shop where orders for paper products could be made which would be freighted to home addresses. Demand was increasing and there would have to be additional staff employed in the near future.

THE PESSA FAMILY BUSINESS – THE WAY FORWARD

H&H Oy (equivalent to a limited company) was set up as the trading name for the papermaking side of the business when the first orders for handmade papers started to come in on a regular basis. The business (as evidenced above) has gone from strength to strength, and Harri and Hanna are keen to continue to expand the business, which has filled a niche in the papermaking industry. In light of the troubling news of a decline worldwide of the pulp and paper industry, Harri and Hanna are acutely aware that they need to increase the production of handmade paper in order to provide sustainability for their forestry business.

The Finnish market has already been comprehensively targeted by H&H Oy, and the first export orders to Norway and Sweden have developed into regular sales. The mind map has produced the analysis of where they are and conclusions for each element of the business had been drawn. According to Harri:

> There is only one way to go, and that is to develop markets in Europe. Look at the success we have had in Norway and Sweden. Let us set up a strategy to market the products in the rest of Europe.

Hanna commented reflectively:

> I don't think that it is going to be as simple as going into neighbouring countries where we have similar working patterns and lifestyles. The session I attended at the business school on Working Across Cultures identified some of the things we would need to consider. I will get the notes from that seminar.

Arriving back at the table, she produced some of the notes that she had taken at the seminar (see Appendices 8.1, 8.2 and 8.3). Harri looked at the notes and responded:

> I agree with you. This does put a different complexion on things. It is a pity that we could not have attended that workshop in Turku on the Etiquette of Business Gift-Giving as I am sure that would have been useful and it was supported by an online guide (<http://www.businessculture.org>) which I am sure could provide the answers to some of our questions.

Harri and Hanna knew that exporting was the most logical step for them to take next. However, it was obvious that they had no idea what products or services they should export or what sales channels they might use. They also needed to know how to set up meetings in different countries and what gifts might be considered appropriate in each country. Indeed, as they talked they realised how little they actually knew about exporting. What they needed to learn initially was "what information should they know about doing business abroad?"

NOTES

[1]This case was prepared by Jane Silver, Professorial Fellow at the University of Salford (UK). It has been prepared as a basis for class discussion rather than to illustrate either the effective or ineffective handing of an administrative situation.

Appendix 8A: **Levels of Culture**

Level of Culture	Method of Discovery	Examples
Artefacts and **Behaviour**	Observation	Architecture, interior design, greetings, rituals, dress, codes of address, business contracts.
Beliefs (statements of fact) and **Values** (preferred statements about the way things should be/ideals)	**Interviews** and **Surveys**	What would be considered as criteria for success? Different stakeholders have different criteria. Beliefs and values differ in terms of what is considered important: product integrity, technological leadership, market share, customer satisfaction or shareholder value. Consider this question: for whom does the company exist? In the USA the response would be the shareholders, in Japan it would be the customers.
Assumptions	**Inference** and **Interpretation**	Kluckhohn and Strodtbeck's Framework (1961) gives a detailed method for analysing cultural environments (see Appendix 8B).

Appendix 8B: **Variations in Value Orientations**

Perception of:	Dimensions			Cultural Dimension
Individual	Good	Good & Evil	Evil	What is the Nature of People?
World	Dominant	Harmony	Sub-jugation	What is a Person's Relationship to Nature?
Human Relations	Individuals	Lateral Groups	Hierar-chical Groups	What is a Person's Relationship to Other People?
Activity	Doing	Controlling	Being	What is the Primary Mode of Activity?

(...Continued on next page)

Appendix 8B (Continued)

Perception of:	Dimensions			Cultural Dimension
Time	Future	Present	Past	What is a Person's Temporal Orientation?
Space	Private	Mixed	Public	What is the Conception of Space?

Source – Table adapted from Kluckhohn and Strodtbeck (1961) *Variations in Value Orientations*, Evanston, IL: Row, Peterson & Company.

NOTE: Further explanations regarding the cultural dimensions are in Appendix 8C.

Appendix 8C: **Cultural Dimensions**

What is the Nature of People?
Cultures differ in how they view each other. High-trust societies leave their doors open and do not expect to be burgled. Low-trust societies count their change after they have made a purchase. In many countries people are more trusting in rural communities than urban centres.

What is a Person's Relationship with Nature?
In agriculture dominance-orientated societies use fertilisers and pesticides to increase crop yield. Harmony-orientated farmers plant the right crops at the right time of year in the right place. Farmers subjugated by nature hope that sufficient rain will fall, but they do not construct irrigation systems. They hope that pests will not attach the crops but they do not use insecticides.

What is a Person's Relationship with Other People?
Personnel policies follow either individual or group orientations. Individual-oriented personnel directors tend to hire those best qualified for the job based on personal skills and expertise. Individualistic applicants will therefore submit applications listing their personal, educational and professional experience. Group-oriented personnel directors also tend to hire those most qualified but their prime qualifications are trustworthiness, loyalty and compatibility with co-workers. They hire friends and relatives of people already working in the organisation. Therefore rather than sending a well-prepared CV applicants look for introductions through family and friends to the managing director.

What is the Primary Mode of Activity?
Doing societies emphasise action; mangers in these societies encourage employees with promotions, pay rises and bonuses. A *being* orientation finds people, ideas and events flowing spontaneously, people stress release, indulgence of existing desires and working for the moment. If

mangers in *being* do not enjoy their job, they leave; they will not work strictly for future rewards. *Control*-orientated societies restrain their desires by detaching themselves from objects in order to allow each person to develop as an integrated whole.

What is a Person's Temporal Orientation?

How do societies use time? Past-oriented cultures believe that plans should be evaluated in terms of their fit with customs and traditions of society, and innovation and change are only justifiable in terms of past experience. Future-oriented cultures believe that they should evaluate plans in terms of the projected future benefits to be gained, and justify innovation and change in terms of the benefits to be gained.

What is the Conception of Space?

How do people use physical space? Is a conference room, an office or a building seen as public or private space? When can I enter an office directly, and when must I wait outside for permission to enter? In some cultures private offices are given to more important employees and important meetings are held behind closed doors. Other societies, however, have no partitions dividing desks; bosses often sit with employees and meeting are attended by everyone.

South Hill Enterprise

THOMAS M. COONEY[1]

Billy Barrett was facing challenges as a consultant that he had never previously experienced. All of the goals that are expected in business practice were not amongst the main priorities here. Confused, he asked Maura Melia, Manager of South Hill Enterprise, if he could clarify the situation.

> Let me see if I've got this right. Excluding the supervisors, each member of staff has some form of intellectual disability. The business has three principal groups of products: chocolate, bakery and preserves (jams). The most profitable of these, and most exciting in terms of market potential, are the chocolate products. However, you do not wish to secure too many large orders for chocolates because the staff would have great difficulty in coping with the increased demand. Additionally, you do not want to focus on chocolates alone because it is important that each member of the staff spends time working on a range of different products as this will enable them to develop a broader range of skills. You want to grow the business, not to make money, but so that you can pay your staff higher wages and employ more people with disabilities. In effect, all of your primary goals are staff-orientated rather than market-orientated.

Maura agreed that this was a good assessment of the situation and wondered what marketing actions could be suggested that South Hill Enterprise should take to help them achieve their goals. Billy wondered also!

BACKGROUND TO SOUTH HILL ENTERPRISE

South Hill Enterprise is a subsidiary of The Sisters of Charity of Jesus and Mary (SCJM), an organisation dedicated to providing care for people with disabilities. South Hill Enterprise was founded in 1993 as a two-year EU Horizon-funded venture. Its primary objective is to provide employment and training opportunities for people with intellectual disabilities. The enterprise was established in St Mary's, South Hill, Delvin, Co. Westmeath, Ireland but moved to an enterprise unit in Athboy, Co. Meath, in May 1994. It is from here that it now employs fourteen people with varying degrees of intellectual disability, in addition to a manager, four supervisors, a part-time administrator and a part-timer driver. Effectively South Hill Enterprise operates as an independent, autonomous operation, although it still remains under the ownership of The Sisters of Charity of Jesus and Mary. However, the initiative is an important element of the overall plan of The Sisters of Charity of Jesus and Mary as it continually seeks to develop a range of innovative community-based services for people with learning disabilities.

South Hill Enterprise produces a wide range of products under three broad product categories: handmade Belgian chocolates, bakery and preserves (see Table 9.1). All of the products are sold under the "South Hill" brand name. The Belgian connection for the chocolates comes via the Horizon Fund's emphasis on promoting collaboration between EU member states and the Sisters' own origins in Flanders, Belgium. The chocolate-making technique employed was developed under personal direction by an expert from Belgium. In addition to supplying chocolates to local retail outlets, South Hill Enterprise also caters for conferences, weddings and corporate gifts. The business additionally supplies chocolates to hamper companies who from time to time include some of the business's other products in their brochures. The handmade chocolate products are primarily distributed to local retail outlets within a 20-kilometre radius, while occasional customers can come from anywhere within the country. Meanwhile, the bakery and preserve products are sold almost exclusively to local retail outlets within the 20-kilometre radius of its production unit.

All of the products are produced to the highest quality control standards through the implementation of HACCP (Hazard Analysis Critical Control Points). South Hill Enterprise also ensures that all hygiene standards are fully met through regular audits and the full implementation of health and safety legislation. In addition to its attention to detail regarding the production processes, only the best quality and freshest ingredients are used in their products. Finally, every member of staff is fully trained to implement the rigid quality control systems within the enterprise.

Table 9.1: **Products Sold by South Hill Enterprises**

Bakery	Preserves (Jams)	Seasonal Bakery/Preserves
Apple Tarts	Strawberry	Rhubarb Chutney
Carrot Cake	Raspberry	Plum Chutney
Coffee Cake	Blackcurrant	Pear Chutney
Rich Fruit	Blackberry	Indian Chutney
Fruit Loaf	Gooseberry	Cucumber Pickle
Fruit Scones	Rhubarb and Ginger	Christmas Cake
Plain Scones	Whiskey Marmalade	Christmas Pudding
Madeira Cake	Three Fruit Marmalade	Plum Pudding Sugar-Free
Tea Brack	Brandy Marmalade	Mince Pies
Whiskey Cake		
Brown Bread		
Chocolate		**Seasonal Chocolate**
480g Box of Chocolates		Easter Eggs
220g Box of Chocolates		Easter Bunnies
170g Box of Chocolates		Easter Hens
65g Box of Chocolates		Chocolate Hare
Box of 1 Chocolate		Santa on a Scooter
Box of 2 Chocolates		Snowman
Loose Chocolates		Christmas Tree

REVIEW OF THE CURRENT SITUATION

Since its inception, the goals of South Hill Enterprise have been quite different to what one would expect from a typical commercial enterprise. Recently the management team revisited the objectives of the enterprise and restated them as follows:

- To provide a safe happy work environment for people with intellectual disabilities

- To create greater awareness of the abilities of people with intellectual disabilities
- To create and maintain close links with local communities
- To generate income for the development of the enterprise
- To provide quality handmade produce for discerning customers

The management team of eight people consists of volunteers and stakeholder representatives who guide the affairs of South Hill Enterprise. The management team meets every two months to review the performance of the business and to determine future actions that need to be taken. Whilst reviewing the objectives of the enterprise, the management team decided that it would be a valuable exercise to also undertake a review of its commercial activities as much of the business that South Hill Enterprise conducts remains seasonal. The busiest times of year tend to be approaching Easter and Christmas when the demand for chocolate products is particularly high. To aid the review process, a study of sales achieved in a three-month period from 15 May to 15 July was analysed. It was thought that this time of year was relatively quieter than other times and that the results would indicate sales without seasonal production having a direct affect. The breakdown of sales according to value was found to be as follows: chocolate 19 per cent, bakery 45 per cent and preserves 36 per cent. However, it was recognised that this would not be a fair reflection of the breakdown of sales on a yearly basis but there were no figures currently available for such an assessment. To begin the investigation into the performance of the business over a twelve-month period, a SWOT analysis (Strengths, Weaknesses, Opportunities and Threats) was undertaken. It was decided that, based upon the results of this analysis, an action plan would need to be developed and implemented. It was at this point that Billy Barrett was invited to act as consultant to the business. His SWOT analysis is given in Table 9.2.

As part of his review of the current situation, Billy noted that the sales figures had improved year-on-year for the past four years, but that a substantial loss was still appearing on the final accounts. Indeed, were it not for the significant financial contribution made annually by The Sisters of Charity of Jesus and Mary South Hill Enterprise would have to close its operations. It surely was not possible for such a situation to continue indefinitely. Billy considered the position and his initial thoughts on solving the problem appeared simple: increase sales, increase margins and reduce costs.

Table 9.2: **SWOT Analysis**

Strengths
• All supervisors have related backgrounds in the food industry. Two of the supervisors have training and work experience in the baking industry.
• All of the supervisors have received training in chocolate production from experts in Belgium.
• Employees are given many opportunities to complete further training.
• All employees are extremely loyal, as are existing customers.
• The support of friends, family and volunteers from the local community is also a great asset.
• Administration support is also readily available from the head office of SCJM in Delvin.
• All products produced by South Hill Enterprise are of the highest quality and the use of machines is minimal. Only fresh ingredients are used in the production of the products (gelatine is not added to the jams, although this is common practice within the industry).
• The chocolates are truly handmade whereas the majority of producers make chocolates that are mass-produced on a production line.
• A strong management team is in operation, which guides the company and makes recommendations on actions to be taken.
• Teamwork is endorsed throughout production. All employees are involved in the decision-making process.
• The proximity of the production unit to Dublin (approximately 50 kilometres) and also to the many towns in the Midlands region means that many customers are within easy reach.
• South Hill Enterprise is a small business, which means that it can be flexible in production.
Weaknesses
• South Hill Enterprise has no planned marketing strategy and there is a lack of funding available for marketing.
• There is no point-of-sales promotion in the customers' outlets.
• South Hill as a brand is not very well established.
• Many people, including the local community, do not know where the business is situated or even that it exists.

(...Continued on next page)

Table 9.2 (Continued)

- South Hill Enterprise does not have an outlet open to the public similar to some of its competitors.

- Customers often comment on the lack of availability of its products in shops. People occasionally telephone the business asking where the products are available for sale (particularly in Dublin). However, the business does not wish to grow to a regional level but rather remain within its broad locality, as it does not have the distribution or manufacturing capability to compete beyond these confines.

- There is no formal distribution system. There is one van that is used to bring the products to the local shops on a once-weekly visit. This van is operated by a driver who has been is employed on a part-time basis.

- While the products are made from the freshest ingredients, this means that they have a shorter shelf-life than some of South Hill's competitors' products, which contain artificial ingredients.

- The main objective of South Hill Enterprise is to provide employment for people with intellectual disabilities. As a result production time takes longer as staff members do not have the same operational capabilities as the employees of its competitors.

- South Hill Enterprise returned a loss on its operations for each of the last four last financial years, despite the support that it received for wages from various government schemes.

- The purchase order requisition system that is in place is slow and bureaucratic. It often means that there is a long lead-time between placing orders, receiving them and suppliers being paid.

- The invoice system that is currently in place is not efficient. Often customers do not pay for the deliveries and do not receive notice of payments due until months later.

- Due to the current workload it is not possible to get all of the administration work completed within a reasonable timeframe.

- Due to financial constraints it is not possible to employ any more people.

- There is a need to determine a new pricing strategy for all of its products as part of a wider marketing strategy. The current pricing is below market averages.

Opportunities

- There is a large market available for each of the three product groups that could be exploited further.

(…Continued on next page)

Table 9.2 (Continued)

- Point-of-sales promotion of the products produced by South Hill Enterprise would create awareness of the company and would help increase sales. A point-of-sales display would also encourage outlets to keep the products in stock and up-to-date.

- Brand development would help create awareness and would also promote customer loyalty. Associations with the brand would be formed – quality, fresh ingredients, handmade and Irish.

- Website redevelopment would help create awareness within the local community and nationwide, show company products and give information to prospective customers.

- Potential target markets consist of retail outlets, corporate bodies, national organisations, hotels, restaurants and coffee shops, government agencies, county and town councils, bridal boutiques, trade fairs and county shows. Other market segments that have not yet been considered are also possible.

- Emphasis could be placed on becoming known as a company that produces hampers for various occasions.

- There is a possibility that a major food manufacturer and distributor would be interested in distributing the chocolate products under the distributor's own brand name and packaging. Discussions have already taken place with one company regarding such a potential alliance.

- There is an opportunity to develop an after-dinner mint as restaurants may be more interested in purchasing an after-dinner chocolate than the current luxurious chocolates.

Threats

- There is a lot of direct and indirect competition in each of the three product groups. There has been strong growth particularly in the number of Irish companies making high-quality chocolate products.

- One of the company's major chocolate competitors has recently relocated to a nearby town.

- Current trends promote healthy living and as a result people may be less willing to purchase luxurious chocolates.

- The significant financial support provided by SCJM cannot be provided indefinitely.

- Each of the three markets is dominated by large national/international companies that have substantial marketing budgets.

EXISTING CUSTOMER SEGMENTS

Defining the customer segments for South Hill products is quite complex as they are available in different markets and through different channels of distribution. The chocolate products are sold to local retailers and also directly to the final consumer anywhere in the country. Meanwhile the bakery and preserve products are sold almost exclusively to local retailers, although some preserve products are bulk-produced for contract sale to other labels. Therefore it is necessary that South Hill Enterprise segments the market and develops multiple marketing strategies. Billy undertook some preliminary profiling of existing consumers and identified a number of clear market segments. These segments serve only as an indicator to the differing needs of the total customer base.

Food Lovers

This segment consists of people who purchase quite frequently. They have a good financial status and prefer to buy a small amount of expensive quality produce rather than a larger quantity of cheaper mass-produced foods. These people enjoy treating themselves and their families. They are inquisitive about new products or good quality products. They enjoy upmarket goods and the prestige that accompanies making the purchase. However, it should be noted that the pricing strategy of South Hill products does not match the premium pricing appropriate for this market segment.

Tourists

Irish handmade and homemade products are becoming increasingly popular with tourists. This segment offers a once-off purchase as they buy in order to have memorabilia of the place that they have just visited. Often this purchase is a gift for somebody else. This segment would apply almost exclusively to the chocolate products but South Hill products are not available in many of the retail outlets frequented by tourists.

Gift Givers

This segment is representative of all socio-economic groups and locations. Purchases are frequently made on impulse with the final decision based on the brand or "look" of the product in the shop. Purchasers are concerned with staying in touch with people and marking occasions, with the benefit gained from making the purchase being admiration and gratitude from the gift receiver. This segment would apply most readily to the chocolate products.

Supporters

This segment is very familiar with the company and may have some connection with the company or its staff (e.g. friends, family). They understand how the company benefits each time they place an order.

Weddings

This is a once-off purchase. The customers in this segment have heard of South Hill chocolates by word of mouth, a trade show, or have seen the chocolates at another wedding. They are looking for something extra special to add to the enjoyment of their day.

Corporate

This segment purchases the products mostly on a once-off basis. They wish to give something back to their customers in order to build customer relations or to give their employees as a form of thanks. This segment is looking for very good quality at a price that is right.

Other Customer Groups

Based on the sales of the company over the past three years, the following customer groups could also be considered:

- Hotels
- Delicatessens
- Hamper companies
- Charity organisations
- Off-License shops
- Car Sales (where a complimentary box of chocolates is included in the purchase of a car)/Garages
- Fruit and vegetable shops

Sales to these groups tend to occur due to random enquiries and little follow-up is ever undertaken with similar types of businesses.

Billy's brief analysis of the different customer groups highlighted two key concerns for him: (1) not enough was known about the profile of each of each the customer groups, and (2) no clear, targeted marketing strategy had been determined for each of these groups. There was a great deal of work ahead of him with regard to this area of activity as he would need to segment the market effectively, and then produce clear goals and action plans for each of the different customer segments. However, he also recognised that he would have to prioritise the actions as the personnel and financial resources were not available to do everything at once.

THE CHOCOLATE MARKET

Statistics show that Ireland has the highest consumption levels of chocolate per capita in Europe after Denmark. The chocolate industry in Ireland was worth approximately €593 million in 2001,[2] with chocolate products accounting for 69 per cent of this, and sugar products accounting for the remaining 31 per cent. Producers in the chocolate and confectionary market vary greatly. Between them the major confectionary manufacturers hold over three-quarters of the market, with Cadburys being the market leader, followed closely by Nestle and Mars. Each of these companies offers a wide range of chocolate products, including boxes of chocolates.

The handmade or traditional chocolate sector is growing in importance in Ireland as consumers now have an interest in buying products that are made in Ireland and have fresh Irish ingredients. These products are also more readily available in shops and the purchase of such chocolates offers consumers a feeling of prestige and luxury. South Hill handmade chocolates are truly handmade but have a shelf-life of just three months due to the fact that the ingredients used are fresh. Many producers of chocolates claim their products are handmade when realistically they are mass-produced. Additionally, their ingredients are not always fresh and therefore they have a longer shelf-life. Currently legislation is attempting to rectify the problem of companies claiming to produce handmade chocolates, which has resulted in many companies now calling their chocolates "handcrafted". There are currently a large number of competitors that produce handmade or handcrafted Irish chocolates and these exist on a national and local basis.

Butlers Chocolates

Butlers' range of chocolates includes bars of chocolates, Irish gift-wrapped selection (500g), chocolate treat selection (125g), deluxe range (750g) and their gift-wrapped ballotin (200g). Butlers also offer a box of two chocolates for weddings and corporate affairs. They provide free delivery with these and the printing of a name or logo is included in the price. Butlers are available nationally and internationally. They supply newsagents, convenience stores and larger supermarkets like Tesco and Dunnes Stores. They also offer sales via their website. Their pricing strategy reflects their premium position in the market.

Lir Chocolates

Lir Chocolates pride themselves on their name, which is derived from the Irish legend of the "Children of Lir". They market themselves as "Premium

Irish Chocolates". Their products consist of Lir exclusive seasonal gift-wrapped collection, Lir golden ballotin, Lir petits fours, the opera box, and Baileys Irish truffles. Lir chocolates are available in newsagents, convenience stores, supermarkets, via their website, in airport shops, and also via their factory shop in Co. Kildare. Their boxes are eye-catching. They also make chocolates with Baileys Irish Cream Liquor, which is a well-known brand of liquor.

Lily O'Brien's

Lily O'Brien's is located in a new custom-designed factory in the heart of Co. Kildare. They describe themselves as suppliers of "high class luxury chocolate to the world". They pride themselves on their "avant garde packaging and remarkably different recipes". Lily O'Brien's are available in newsagents, convenience stores and larger supermarkets. They are also available on their website and also from their factory shop in Kildare. Lily O'Brien's are also sold in airport shops where they do special promotional deals such twin packs.

PRESERVES INDUSTRY

It is estimated that the total preserves and spreads market in Ireland is worth approximately €38.3 million. Marmalade and jam are by far the most significant segments of this category, accounting for €14.2 million and €12.9 million respectively. It is thought that year-on-year sales of marmalade are now static but the market is still significant. The market for good quality home-produced jams continues to grow while the market for commercially produced jams is in decline. The growth of home-produced jams is due to the fact that they are free from artificial colourings and generally have a higher fruit content. The sale of relishes and chutneys to catering and industrial users, in particular to sandwich bars and restaurants, has also increased. However, this increase has not yet followed through at the retail level. South Hill Enterprise homemade jam is free from artificial colourings and preservatives and has a high fruit percentage. It is in direct competition with national jam producers and also with individuals who produce homemade jams.

Fruitfield Foods

The Fruitfield jam and marmalade recipes can be traced all the way back to 1853 when the Lamb brothers started making jams and marmalades for the Irish market. Fruitfield claims to be the dominant brand in the market with a 52.6 per cent share of sales. It produces "Old Time" marmalade (the single biggest-selling marmalade in Ireland), and it also produces diabetic and sugar-free marmalades. The company invests substantially in strong brand promotion.

Chivers

Chivers has been producing jam in Ireland for over seventy years. There are eleven flavours within the Chivers jam range. These include strawberry, raspberry, blackcurrant, apricot, gooseberry, pineapple, strawberry and apple, seedless raspberry, bramble jelly, mixed fruit, and lemon curd. All their jams are fat-free and made without any artificial colours, flavours and preservatives. They are generally regarded as being the second strongest player in the market.

Folláin Jams

"Folláin" is the Irish word for wholesome. Folláin is a successful indigenous Irish company based in West Cork producing a range of jams and preserves. Their jams are made from natural home-grown fruit, handpicked in local fields and hedgerows in the clear unpolluted climate of West Cork. A number of the Folláin jams have won awards from the Guild of Fine Food Retailers.

Bonne Maman

Bonne Maman is a premium French jam, which has been the uncontested leader in its market with a continuing strategy to sustain growing consumer demand. Its homemade image appears very attractive to the customer. Its jams are 100 per cent natural and are free from artificial colouring, preservatives and flavourings. The brand is beginning to make a significant impact in the Irish market.

BAKERY

The Irish cake market has been increasing steadily in recent times and in 2001 was worth approximately IR£55 million.[3] The following factors are driving the growth of the cake sector: increased heavier buyers, increased penetration from 81 per cent to 85 per cent, increased spend of IR£11.80 to IR£13.10, increased average price per cake from IR£1.48 to IR£1.58, and a yearly growth of 3.6 per cent. The market is broken down into private labels worth IR£15 million and branded cakes worth IR£40 million. Gateaux claim 13 per cent of the branded cake market, followed by O'Hara with approximately 7 per cent and Mr Kipling with 5 per cent. South Hill Enterprise is in direct competition with these national producers as well as with regional bakeries that produce fresh cake products on a daily basis. For example, Spicers and O'Reillys are strong regional companies that supply retailers with goods similar to those under the South Hill brand. However, they have a competitive advantage as they additionally supply large quantities of bread to such shops, making it convenient for retailers to also stock their cakes. Additionally there is a local bakery situated on the main street in Athboy, which is much more convenient than the premises for South Hill Enterprise. They produce a wide range of cakes and benefit from impulse purchases from customers who visit their shop.

PROMOTIONAL STRATEGY

The promotional strategy of South Hill Enterprise has generally incorporated trade shows, which have generated some business for the chocolate products, sporadic cold calls to retailers to introduce them to the South Hill range of products, and word of mouth, which has been the most successful form of promotion. There have been some attempts to develop free publicity through the local radio stations and weekly newspapers, but this has never been sustained. The most successful media campaign occurred when South Hill Enterprise won a national O2 Ability Award for companies employing people with disabilities and so the business had "a story to tell". Many ideas for a promotional strategy have been discussed but a coordinated campaign has not yet been implemented. Part of the challenge to introducing any campaign is the identification of clear goals for the promotional activity, since the objectives identified by the management team for the business are quite diverse.

As part of the review process by the management team it was determined that there was a fundamental requirement to change the packaging of the chocolate products so as to present a more upmarket, handmade, high quality image. The jars for the preserves were changed in January 2007 to reflect such an image, as previously the jars were plain and did not stand out from other jams on the shelf. There was also a requirement to change the labels on the jars, as they also looked too commercial and gave out a mass-produced image of the product. All preserve products are now being sold in the new octagon shaped jars and have the new labels attached. The writing on the label is in a handwritten style giving the image of homemade produce. However, the chocolate boxes remain in plain white boxes with just a small gold label giving the brand name. To improve the image of the products, it was decided that the boxes should be gift-wrapped by the employees as part of the packaging process. This gives the chocolate products a high quality finish and a greater prospect of impulse purchase as it saves the customer from having to gift-wrap the chocolates themselves. An additional benefit of this process is that it provides employees with a new task, thereby expanding the range of skills being developed at a personal level. The disadvantage to the process inevitably is that it is slow and very time-consuming.

The management team have also recognised the need for promotional material in the form of a brochure. A new logo has been designed for the South Hill brand and this will be used in all promotional material. There is also a need to develop a newsletter/leaflet that could be sent to all businesses within a 20-kilometre radius. This could help create awareness about the business, as many people from the locality do not even know of its existence. This campaign could be carried out on an annual basis and could be incorporated as an activity for volunteers. Another idea discussed was to develop a new promotional "tag" which could be a nice small piece of quality cardboard tied around the neck of the jam jars with twine. On the front of this tag would be the company name, etc. while overleaf would be a recipe into which the jams or chutneys might be incorporated. It is suggested that this promotional activity be carried out in line with the changing seasons. This idea could be further supported by providing retailers with a wooden-based stand so that all of the South Hill products could be grouped together. It may be possible to approach local schools, sheltered workshops, prisons, etc. that provide woodwork as a subject to ask them to produce such stands.

There have been many more ideas explored under the heading of "promotional strategy". However, any campaign must be cognisant of the following limitations:

- Little finance is available to spend on a promotional campaign so it needs to be a guerrilla-styled promotional campaign.
- There are limited personnel available to work on the campaign as the supervisors and manager are currently working to their full capacity simply to meet existing orders.
- It is important that the campaign generates business equally across the three different product ranges so that a broad range of skills can be developed by the employees.
- It would not be possible to meet any explosion in demand and therefore sales generation has to be managed carefully.
- The campaign must recognise all of the objectives of the business identified by the management team.

As Billy Barrett reviewed these limitations, what initially appeared to be a simple solution to improving the sales situation of the business was suddenly becoming far more complex! The campaign would have to be layered in such a way that it would build momentum on a slow continuous basis. This ruled out any prospect of using fast-acting remedies since South Hill Enterprise could not react effectively to unexpected large demands. It was also difficult for the business to build up a stock of goods as the shelf-life of the products was quite short and warehousing space was very limited.

Pricing Strategy

Billy Barrett also undertook some basic market research to investigate the prices of the competitors' products. It was found that South Hill products were less expensive than most of its competitors, usually about 20 per cent below the average price for a product. It was clearly evident from the research that a future pricing strategy needed to be established. This new strategy needed to be based on the amount competitors were charging for similar products and also on the amount that South Hill believed its customers would be willing to pay. The price would also need to reflect the quality of the products that it offered. He also noted that the margin for South Hill chocolate products was far higher than that being achieved with the South Hill bakery and preserve products, and again he was tempted to focus on the chocolate products alone.

As part of the review of the pricing strategy, Billy also examined the accounts for the business and found that there was very little room to reduce costs as the business was being run very frugally. Labour costs were low due to government support schemes, general overheads were reasonable, and material costs were above average due to the high quality ingredients that South Hill uses in its products. Overall it meant that there was little room to reduce costs but there was substantial opportunity to increase the margins on all of the products. The biggest challenge was to determine how great a price increase could be introduced and how the retailers and consumers would react. Maybe any price increases would have to be done on a phased basis until they had reached the appropriate pricing point for South Hill products.

What to Do?

This assignment was turning into one of the most difficult jobs of Billy's consultancy career. With financial backing, much could be achieved for the business but there was no organisation or state agency that could provide such help. Whatever was going to be done had to be achieved with the resources that were currently available. An increase in prices would help but he needed to work out how that could be achieved most effectively. The chocolate boxes needed to be improved but that would mean additional costs. A coherent promotional campaign needed to be developed but there was no one available to undertake the substantial amount of work required to do it properly. The campaign would have to be very carefully managed so that there were no sudden bursts in sales with which the company could not cope. However, production was very seasonal and he needed to find some way of levelling the production output throughout the year with products that had a short shelf-life. There was no salesperson for the business and the driver was employed on a part-time basis. There was no coherent marketing strategy and yet one was urgently required. However, even with a clear marketing strategy, who would implement it? Everyone in the organisation was working to their full ability and no individual or group of individuals could be faulted in any way for their performance. This was the way in many small businesses.

South Hill Enterprise had recently received a request to meet a large food distributor who wanted to talk to them about making products for the distributor's label. This opportunity would solve many of the problems faced by South Hill Enterprise, but a different set of difficulties would then arise for the business. The food distributor would not be understanding of the needs of the employees and any deadlines having to be met could cause intolerable stress for everyone involved in South Hill Enterprise. Was it worth making a major change in how the business operated, or could Billy find solutions within the existing business practice?

NOTES

[1] This case was developed by Thomas M. Cooney, who is Director of the Institute for Minority Entrepreneurship at the Dublin Institute of Technology. It has been prepared as a basis for class discussion rather than to illustrate either effective or ineffective handling of a business situation.

[2] *Checkout* magazine, November 2001.

[3] The figures given here are from a quote in *Checkout* magazine (November 2001) by Stephen Bannon, Marketing Manager for Hibernia Foods (distributors of Entenmann's Cakes).

Hytec

RICKIE A. MOORE AND OLIVIER TORRES[1]

While Hytec began its operations as a solo (micro) enterprise, it grew quickly and generated extensive activity in the global market. From its earliest days, the business was driven by a passionate individual (Jean-Jacques Promé) in a never-ending search for entrepreneurial innovation and technological entrepreneurship. In fact, Hytec's success is arguably the result of its solid entrepreneurial foundation and leadership, plus its strong innovation. However, the current CEO of Hytec (Pierre Emmanuel Gaillard) realised that the company was approaching a critical point in its history. Although exports had been increasing steadily since 2000 and now accounted for 66 per cent of Hytec's annual sales (driven primarily by Hytec's constant innovative activity), the cost of sales was rising and the majority of its sales force did not belong to Hytec. With an exhaustive and impressive range of innovative products, was it time for Hytec to make a quantum leap and adopt a global entrepreneurship approach to its technology and innovation? If so, how should they go about it? Global sales might be one thing, but global entrepreneurship in technology and innovation for a small enterprise (SME) is quite another.

ENTREPRENEURIAL BEGINNING

Hytec, short for HydroTechnology, is a small business in Montpellier, France, that employs approximately forty people. Initially, the business started off by specialising in the detection of cracks in the deep-sea pipelines of offshore oil platforms, based on the considerable experience and knowledge of the founder, Jean-Jacques Promé. An electronics engineer with basic training, Jean-Jacques was undaunted by two previous start-ups that resulted in bankruptcies (bailiffs had even seized his personal belongings to auction them in order to repay the debts). Not being very wealthy at that time, Jean-Jacques' furniture was not worth very much. All his tools and equipment were seized and sold and anything that was deemed to be of any value was confiscated. With the sky falling on his head, and a gutted apartment, Jean-Jacques and his family passed through a very difficult period in their lives. However, with some financial backing from his grandfather, Jean-Jacques succeeded in convincing a group of friends and colleagues (who were all either engineers or technicians) to join him in the venture. And so with great enthusiasm Jean-Jacques created and launched HydroTechnology in 1981, with one of his friends as the "frontman" and CEO.

Jean-Jacques Promé had a passion for the sub-aquatic world and was fascinated in exploring it, not only for its pristine beauty, but also in being able to share the treasures of the dark and deep (inaccessible to many) through an innovative combination of cameras and television. He was also motivated by the industrial applications of his technology as he could film and relay sub-aquatic industrial processes such as boring, drilling and other activities. From the outset, he had sensed the emergence of a remote surveillance market, and was convinced that the market would blossom in the future and that there would be a need for its numerous applications.

Jean-Jacques had a knack for capturing and displaying images, and developed television camera systems that would film entire uninterrupted sequences, rather than just take pictures and capture images of specific operations or stages. Combining a basic video recorder and an external camera, Jean-Jacques identified his competitive advantage and added value as being able to not only film entire processes, but also to relay the information (film) directly to a command station some distance away. He had built his first series of prototypes in his bedroom in the small family apartment that he had rented in Montpellier. Next, needing more space, he progressively occupied the sitting room, the dining room and then he transformed his tiny garage (large enough to accommodate his matchbox Citroen 4L) into his workshop where he produced the first set of devices. Later on he would rent a somewhat larger apartment and utilise the garden shed as his workshop.

In parallel, Jean-Jacques had also started his family and the birth of his two sons occurred during the formative years of Hytec. Throughout all the trials and tribulations his wife Genevieve (who was pursuing her studies in medicine) and his in-laws (who were from a middle-class family) stuck with and supported him. He had succeeded in winning over his in-laws, who initially had resented the fact that their daughter had married a working-class man; they admired his drive and determination. Jean-Jacques had been black-listed by the Bank of France, and was not allowed to own and operate a personal bank account anywhere in France. No bank, investor nor enterprise would offer him any credit as he was legally classified as un-creditworthy. He could not receive any subventions from any governmental institutions or programs. All doors were closed to him.

> It was psychologically very devastating – I was ruined. Genevieve had always supported me in my endeavours and in this very difficult moment she trusted me completely. I could never have continued my dream if Genevieve was fighting with me at home in the midst of all the problems. A serene and quiet family life is very important – it helps to balance the stress of work. She stuck by and with me and remained a key supporter throughout, even though her friends were encouraging her to think about her own security and that of Guillaume and Christophe [their sons]. In all honesty, Genevieve never tried to make me change my mind or to give up my dream. Together we rode through the storm. Prohibited from owning a company but not from working for a living, I did all sorts of odd jobs to earn money to clear my debts with the governmental institutions – social security, tax, etc. I could not repay everyone and chose to forsake my creditors.

Among his many products and services, Jean-Jacques had also specialised in the installation of closed-circuit television (CCTV) systems that would allow his clients to effectively and efficiently monitor their properties and directly observe all movement and actions at their locations. As part of his R&D (research and development) programme, Jean-Jacques also invented his first explosive-proof, anti-inflammable camera that could operate in highly volatile environments without producing ignition due to friction or interaction with the environment. In building his explosive-proof camera, Jean-Jacques had used basic ingredients, including enhanced high velocity nitrogen and medical nanometers.

Hytec's mission was to design and manufacture remote control systems for televisual inspection and intervention in "hostile environments" (i.e. places that are either inaccessible to humans or where human intervention would pose very significant safety risks or be extremely costly). Initially, a significant portion of Hytec's customer base consisted of deep-sea oil-drilling companies with offshore platforms spread throughout the oceans of the world. In this market (remote controlled underwater video cameras) the surveillance and maintenance of deep-sea pipelines requires ad hoc customised technical solutions for which the classic product offering was inadequate. The innovation of the technical solutions and systems designed and developed by Hytec allowed it to satisfy an increasing number of specialised and customised orders, develop its global sales and diversify its devices and fields of application.

Today Hytec has many fields of expertise, from electronics and mechanics to industrial information technology and optics. But aside from its technological prowess and R&D, Hytec has a strong need for commercial and management skills (especially in cost analysis), as it is often required to quickly analyse the specifications of each custom order so as to make an accurate estimate for each particular service. Given the specialisation of this market and the nature of the activity, a highly competent sales force is indispensable for firms such as Hytec to survive. So far Hytec has relied almost exclusively on a highly qualified and perfectly mobile senior management team for its development to date. According to Jean-Jacques:

> It is true. Judging by the almost systematic articles in the media that we got after every operation, the most interesting aspect of our performances, associated with the areas in which we work, was that they produced a certain notoriety with the public. Beyond this very pleasurable brand image it was through a desire to make constant progress towards high technology products capable of responding to, and pushing back the limits of, human intervention in hostile environments that Hytec positioned itself in the market and intended to play a key role.

FINANCING CREATIVITY AND INNOVATION AT HYTEC

The development of Hytec (a constant increase of 40 per cent in its turnover per annum) has not been without its challenges. While Hytec has had no problem in raising capital (increasing its share capital six times and now amounting to a consolidated €427,000), Hytec's growth was such that the structure of the initial organisation was no longer able to keep up with the increase in demand, both in France and overseas. A number of organisational changes were implemented and a new structure was thus set up, including: (1) the creation of a mechanical subsidiary (Hymatec), (2) the renewal of the equipment for the R&D workshops and the manufacturing and production department, (3) the computerisation of all of the firms' operations, (4) the hiring of new technical, sales and commercial representatives and executives, and (5) with its new size and expansion Hytec moved to new premises. By strengthening its technical, technological, commercial and administrative means, Hytec's brand image was reinforced internationally. Jean-Jacques Promé and his team also took the decision to open up Hytec's share capital, and to register the company on the off-board market on the Marseille stock exchange. The financial director explained:

> Should we have avoided the stock exchange, knowing that it is a dangerous business for an SME? In fact, we did not have much choice. Our investments had soon become very high, with a high point of €230,000 just three years after the creation of the company. It was a level that could not be maintained with the initial capital of €15,000. We quickly had to raise the capital in agreement with the founder and two new associates, raising it first to €76,000 and then to €122,000. An input of new money was nevertheless necessary to keep up with the increased needs for operating capital. Hytec appealed to two venture capital investors. A further increase in capital still turned out to be insufficient. It was then that we first talked about floating the company on the stock market but, as we were not big enough for the second market, we were floated on the off-board. This enabled us to have a further input of new money. Floating the company was essential to giving us a new lease of life.

ENTREPRENEURIAL OPPORTUNITIES

The year after its floatation Hytec recorded its biggest contract in the nuclear sector. Hytec signed a contract worth more than €3 million with Sonatrach in Algeria for the cleansing of four galleries of water supply of the gas liquefaction GL1Z and GL2Z. The experience gained by Hytec over twenty-five years through various equivalent building sites was a dominating criterion in the final choice. For this work, Hytec designed the VISIT, a remote controlled vehicle of approximately six tons. It was composed of two electro-hydraulic power stations (propulsion and tools) and a number of cameras and sensors that assisted the operators. It was connected to the control unit via an electro-mechanical umbilical cable 500 metres long. The VISIT enabled the immerged galleries to be cleaned in order to restore the flow necessary for the full operation of the gas liquefaction units. However, the work for Sonatrach actually got started nine months behind schedule, and financially Hytec was hit hard by this delay. Jean-Jacques Promé also approached ANVAR (the French national agency for promoting research) to support the development and construction of ERICA (an internal repair kit for pipelines). With these new devices designed to cleanse sea water supply galleries, Hytec placed itself in the environmental and pipelines markets. Hytec was also aware of the potential that its broader knowledge would have for these markets, and so it additionally developed a number of remote controlled systems for video inspection of sewerage networks, the cleansing of galleries and the remote manipulation of toxic waste.

By 2005 Hytec had clearly established itself as a major global player in three sectors: (1) off-shore drilling and sub-aquatic exploration, (2) the nuclear sector and (3) pipe and sewerage operations. Its growing international fame skyrocketed with two world-famous events. Firstly, Hytec gained significant international publicity from the role that its custom-built *Robin* robot played in exploring and inspecting the wreckage of the *Titanic*. Attached to the underside of the *Nautile*, the *Robin* was perhaps the world's smallest robotic remote controlled high-definition video camera capable of transmitting its images live to a control station at the surface of the ocean. Measuring 60cm^3, the *Robin* was invented by Jean-Jacques Promé himself. The *Robin* meandered its way around the interior of the ship, filming its grand staircase, the engines, dining hall, cabins, etc. Over the fifty-four day expedition period, the *Robin* would show the *Titanic* to the world. *Robin* offered exceptional functionality (including sideways movement), and a Side Scan Sonar System that no other remote operated vehicle (ROV) offered at that time. Tethered to its mothership (the *Nautile*), *Robin* had a 4,00 metre umbilical cord, and was used extensively to film over 140 hours of video footage and 7,000 still images of the inside of the wreck and its surroundings. Today, the *Robin* is still in active service in France.

Some years later, Oscar Academy Award-winning director James Cameron directed and filmed the groundbreaking cinematic achievement. Cameron journeyed back to the site of the legendary wreck of the *Titanic*, and explored the entire ship, deck by deck, room by room, encountering mysteries that remained hidden for almost a century, all with the help of the *Robin*. The movie *Titanic* would go on to win an Oscar, and Hytec was presented to the world as a specialist in the miniaturization of ROVs and remote control systems for televisual inspection and intervention in "hostile environments".

Over the course of Hytec's expansion the company has been forced to broaden its range of activities and its innovations. From initially specialising in interventions in deep-sea sub-aquatic environments, particularly for the oil industry, the company decided to diversify into the nuclear sector so that they would not be totally dependent on the oil industry. Jean-Jacques Promé was conscious of the impact and global fallouts of the two oil crises that led to the cessation of all drilling programmes on the platforms owned by the world's leading oil companies. At the time, the nuclear sector was a totally exploitable escape route as it had similar characteristics to the oil sector. Nuclear activities are another area where certain forms of human intervention are impossible. It was at this point that the company's real mission started to become clear. Within a few years, Hytec succeeded in taking a significant market share in the televisual equipment and remote controlled maintenance tools markets. Once again, the considerable slowdown in the French nuclear programme, and the problems of penetrating this "sensitive" sector abroad, led the managerial team to identify another hostile environment. This time it was the pipe and sewerage market, and notably the water supply line market, that seemed to offer great potential. It appears that although the professions within the company are based on the mastery and combination of varied, highly specialised know-how, its mission can be simply summarised as being based on the concept of "hostile milieus", that is, environments that are inaccessible to humans or where human intervention is unsafe, unreasonably costly and potentially fatal. Hytec's growth came from a succession of diversifications in its clientele, whilst always aiming to satisfy the same type of targeted needs.

TECHNOLOGICAL INNOVATION AND ENTREPRENEURSHIP AT HYTEC: BETWEEN EVOLUTION AND REVOLUTION

The perpetual evolution of technological innovation and entrepreneurship were always the hallmarks of Hytec. Successfully satisfying clients who required more engineering, technology and innovation in their devices, Hytec quickly recognised that its future lay in these domains. Hytec's miniature camera products testify to this unweaving drive to find highly innovative solutions to the challenges faced by clients. For a long time, cameras had undergone a relatively moderate evolution. With the arrival of the mass-consumer camcorder, the world of image recording and filming would be revolutionised. As the cameras became more sophisticated and miniaturised, they also acquired new properties and became resistant to radiation, flame proof, pressure resistant, etc. Hytec seized the opportunity presented by the camera revolution and combined it with robotics and remote control mechanisms. Jean-Jacques Promé was able to perfect his ideas and invented a new remote controlled and robotic inspection camera.

However, the industrial evolutions kept emerging. Clients no longer wanted only just images but also measurement. Sonar and ultrasound technologies soon found their way into Hytec's devices. On the next wave, Hytec was able to propose cameras that evaluated the degree of erosion and certain industrial risks. But Hytec did not stop there. Drawing upon the evolutions in information technology, computers and software, Hytec was able to integrate all of these evolutions to manufacture devices that allowed its clients to not only have images, measurement and information, but also knowledge derived from information that was processed and interpreted by artificial intelligence systems and intelligent software.

Elsewhere, an inventor from Montpellier had invented a system to separate solid particles from wine and eliminate 95 per cent of the impurities, thus resulting in a better quality product. The system had one drawback in that its microscopic pores in the filtration membrane had to be constantly washed as they were blocked frequently. A professor from the local university came up with a solution to the membrane problem and filed a patent. The local branch of the University and Enterprise Partnership for Business Development supported the professor and financed the development and fabrication of a prototype machine that would purify wastewater. The prototype (with a low consumption of energy, not too big, and not too heavy) was manufactured by Hytec. It was 1.2 metres high and weighed 50 kilograms. Enthusiastically, Jean-Jacques Promé and the professor went to Bolivia to demonstrate their machine to the local elected officials, in the presence of journalists. In selecting the filthiest and most polluted of rivers with a dead dog floating in it, Jean-Jacques Promé proceeded with the demonstration. The odour of the pollution was so strong and repulsive that even the officials could not stand it. After a few minutes, the machine filled a glass with the purified water and the professor drank it with pleasure as though it was a glass of Grand Cru Bordeaux wine. The media coverage of the demonstration was extensive.

Jean-Jacques Promé never believed in patents. As a subcontractor for a large international water treatment firm he conceived a pliable and expandable machine to be used in cleaning constricted and blocked water and sewerage galleries. However, the negotiations between the contracting company and its client broke down, and the engagement of Hytec was halted. Determined to protect his invention, Jean-Jacques Promé filed a patent application. Promé pursued his idea and using a number of sketchings and a film he was able to convince the contracting firm to reopen negotiations with its client. The client was convinced and awarded the contract to the company, and Hytec was engaged to build the machine.

Hytec was able to sell several of the machines even though it did not have a real sales force.

MISSED OPPORTUNITY

Hytec was probably the first company to invent a miniaturised camera with a hemispheric screen. For this, Jean-Jacques Promé regrets that he did not file a patent for it. Millions of these cameras have today been sold and are in use in airports, shops, supermarkets, museums, etc., and are used for the protection of individuals and property. His invention was really simple. By positioning Hytec in the niche for intervention in hostile environments it was important to conceive smaller and smaller, and more resistant and high performance cameras. Realising that a camera only films what is in front of its objective (sometimes protected by a flat screen) Jean-Jacques Promé figured that if he had installed a motorisation mechanism, he could move the entire camera and thus increase its vision. However, this meant motorising the camera's axis in a very small and confined space, and so the camera needed to have the space for the motor. Additionally, if the camera could move, it also meant that the protective screen had to move as well. After many brainstorming sessions, Jean-Jacques Promé developed the idea to use a hemispheric screen as opposed to a flat one. Within the hollow of the hemisphere, the camera and the objective could stay pivoted or move in all directions. Whatever the position of the hemisphere (vertical or horizontal), the camera had a large space in which to manoeuvre. As a single "mono bloc" device, there was no external movement as all movement was confined and contained within the hemisphere. Today, Hytec uses this system on most of its devices. Hytec's competitors took some six years to imitate Hytec and the system is currently generalised and commonplace.

CHANGING OF THE GUARD

With the increasing success of Hytec, Jean-Jacques had received several offers to sell his company but he always refused. He felt that he could not allow Hytec to be run by someone who was foreign to the culture and philosophy that he had worked so hard to nurture and embed in Hytec. In January 2000, nearing retirement age and wanting to spend more time on his technology and innovation hobbies but without the pressure of managing the company, Jean-Jacques finally accepted an offer from an engineering industrialist (specialising in mechanical, hydraulic, electronic and information engineering and design, optics, magnetism, etc.) to buy his shares. In July 2000 the deal was signed and as part of it, Jean-Jacques agreed to remain as the CEO for a period of three years minimum (four years maximum, until his replacement was named), he would help recruit his successor, and he would be hired as a consultant for those projects and orders where Jean-Jacques felt he could be useful. The industrialist, a fervent believer in technology and innovation, also promised to significantly boost Hytec's R&D in terms of equipment and increase its technical staff, and to extend Hytec's collaboration with various technology research organisations, laboratories and universities.

With the announcement of the sale, anxiety set in. Everyone wondered what would be the future of Hytec. Jean-Jacques spent much of his time trying to reassure the employees that life would go on as before. However, many were still very anxious. The new owners of Hytec thought of hiring a "manager" to replace Jean-Jacques, as no one at Hytec had any prior experience in running a multi-million high-tech SME and managing thirty employees. Throughout the search process (transition period) Jean-Jacques maintained the close contact that he had with every employee and continued to lead as though nothing had changed. He was still very active in all the projects and kept pushing the development of newer and newer technologies and innovations. The outcome of the search process resulted in Pierre-Emmanuel Gaillard's appointment as CEO in 2004. Pierre-Emmanuel had been hired by Jean-Jacques since he graduated from university. With a masters degree, Pierre-Emmanuel joined Hytec in September 1989, starting off as an electronic engineer and an information technology technician. One year later, he became the Head of Electronics. Moving further up the ladder, Pierre-Emmanuel became the Director of R&D and Technical Operations within two years of joining Hytec. Pierre-Emmanuel's appointment to the top job was also reassuring for the staff.

Their anxiety following the sale of Jean-Jacques' shares was instantly relieved and the internal pressure that had built up dropped immediately. Pierre-Emmanuel had worked closely with Jean-Jacques and he knew the company inside out. Once the sale of Jean-Jacques' shares had been signed, he had also started assisting Jean-Jacques with sales and the management of the firm. In 2004, some two decades after the creation of the company, and at forty years of age, Pierre-Emmanuel took over the reins of Hytec. The transition had been smooth, efficient and uneventful. As part of the negotiations, Pierre-Emmanuel obtained an agreement that Hytec would continue to operate almost in total autonomy as it did before, that Hytec would continue in its technological/innovation trajectory, and that he would retain all of the staff, boost its R&D, and develop its brand and product image. In exchange, Pierre-Emmanuel agreed to develop Hytec's sales and to take the company to the next level. Confident in Pierre-Emmanuel's abilities and having kept his end of the sale deal, Jean-Jacques was finally able to begin his new life – spending more time with his family, pursuing his leisure activities, but still around and assisting where needed. As a result, the organisational change at Hytec was minimal.

GLOCAL SALES

One of Hytec's strengths was its ability to serve both its national and international markets. However, useful and pertinent market data concerning Hytec's segments was not easy to obtain. Realistic market demand data beyond general macroeconomic ones, both nationally and internationally, was a distant utopia and a complicated game of deduction and extrapolation. In the offshore oil industry, customers were mostly large established companies (often global operators), and the market was extremely fragmented. In the nuclear market, it was totally the opposite as operators were few and were mostly centralised governmental organisations. Customers were most often the governments themselves and they would organise their procurement through a tendering or bidding process. Hytec would rival national laboratories and research organisations and the bidding process was long, expensive and exhausting. Moreover, results were not guaranteed, and because of the bidding process margins could be either zero or very low, and there was no way to increase prices once the tender had been approved and accepted. In terms of the nuclear market, it was sensitive to national legislation (various restrictions and opportunities) and often the subject of international pressure from political action groups such as Greenpeace and local citizens opposed to nuclear energy. While many of the owners and operators of the pipe industry were private companies, most of the sewerage operators were either local or territorial governments. According to Pierre-Emmanuel Gaillard:

> Figuring out where they stood was no easy matter. We would need to monitor their maintenance or overhaul plans. Anyway, once a local authority would have bought one of our devices, they will not necessarily repurchase several others, as they will use the device extensively throughout their networks. And with our extended warranty plans, if something goes wrong we will repair the device. Even if several devices were needed at once, most would rent rather than buy them. Our devices were long-term investments.

By 2005 Hytec was generating approximately one-third of its revenues in each of the three sectors, and its product mix consisted of approximately 60 per cent standard products and 40 per cent custom-built. Hytec had clearly diversified its sales. The new trend was towards a fifty/fifty mix driven by the international orders. Pierre-Emmanuel Gaillard was aware of the challenges and opportunities he faced concerning each segment of the market. Each segment was different, at different stages in their respective markets, the sales processes differed, and custom orders were a double-edged sword (see Table 10.1).

Table 10.1: **Hytec's Three Sectors**

Offshore		Nuclear	Water		
Oil (80%)	Oceanogra-phy (20%)	Nuclear (100%)	Sanitisa-tion (70%)	Drilling (25%)	Large Hydraulic Projects (5%)

Export business accounted for 66 per cent of its sales and was growing yearly, with Hytec products being sold in forty-five countries around the world. With an army of sales representatives in over twenty countries, Hytec was selling its equipment either directly or through local agents, who provided after-sales service in the country where the equipment was used. Hytec also provided technical assistance to customers around the world (start-up and maintenance of equipment, training of operators). In some countries there were even multiple agents. Pierre Emmanuel Gaillard was categorical – "the agents make all decisions". However, none of them had a contract with Hytec and many even sold competing products. So far, all his relationships with these agents had been based on trust. Through the custom orders, Hytec was also expanding its product range, and the new demands for miniaturised devices were requiring whole new competences and processes that Hytec had to decide whether to appropriate or to obtain through subcontracting.

INDUSTRIAL SECTORS AND COMPETITION

Off-shore oil exploration is directly dependent on the price of a barrel of crude oil. As the price increases the conditions and requirements for drilling and exploration improve and become more lucrative. In the aftershock of an oil crisis or with an increase in the exchange rate of the dollar, much attention is given to the nuclear sector as a substitute for a global dependence on oil. The continued increase in the price of a barrel of oil since late 2004 and the breaking of the psychological barrier of $60-a-barrel in June 2005 had been a blessing for Hytec as renewed attention was turned to nuclear sources of energy. Strictly speaking, Hytec does not have a competitor anywhere in the world that is identical. However, on each segment, it has a number of competitors (see Table 10.2).

Table 10.2: **Competitors**

Offshore	Nuclear	Water
Kongsberg (Nor) Benthos (US) ROS (US) Seaeye (UK)	Rees IST (US) Raditech (GB) QI (Jap) Cyberia (Fra) Diakont (Rus) VIT (US)	IPEK (Aus) Hydrovidéo (Fra) ROV developpement (Fra) IBAK (Ger) Rausch (Ger) RICO (Ger) CUES (US) Inuktum (Can)

It is interesting to note that the management of Hytec knew many of their competitors very well as they some were former employees of Hytec. "We often meet at the expositions and discuss our industries", declared Pierre-Emmanuel Gaillard. Each segment functions like an oligarchy where price is not necessarily the decisive factor but innovation and interpersonal relationships (trust, reliability, etc.) between clients and suppliers is critical. In some segments (such as nuclear), one sells not only technology, but also confidence, surety and security. Most of Hytec's competitors are also SMEs and they also try to differentiate themselves by their reputation.

BOARD MEETING

Pierre-Emmanuel was deep in thought. Fully aware of Hytec's strengths he wondered whether Hytec was overly innovative. While sales were good (€5 million per annum) and the company was stable, what opportunities lay ahead for Hytec? Hytec was definitely a market leader but could Hytec better leverage its technologies and its innovations? For each option that came to mind, Pierre-Emmanuel realised that Hytec did not necessarily have access to all of the various networks that would make Hytec part of the chosen solution, even though Hytec had some knowledge of the particular market. There was also one variable that Hytec did not master – politics; national politics did not necessarily align with regional politics, and sometimes even clashed with that of other countries. How should he lead the meeting as much had to be decided. Where should he start?

NOTES

[1]This case was prepared by Rickie Moore and Olivier Torres of EM LYON, France. It has been prepared as a basis for class discussion rather than to illustrate either the effective or ineffective handling of an administrative situation.

Hytec

Appendix 10A: **Hytec's Range of Products**

Hytec has an extensive range of standardised products split into three categories and a number of custom-built devices:

Segment	Products
Underwater Segment	13 TV Cameras and Lights 3 Pan and Tilt Units and Manipulators 5 Remote Controlled Vehicles 5 Custom Built Devices
Nuclear	18 TV Cameras and Lights 5 Pan and Tilt Units and Manipulators 5 Telesurveillance Networks 5 Carriers 5 Custom-Built Devices
Pipe and Borehole	13 Sewerage Systems 3 Water and Supply Networks 1 Small Pipe Inspection Device 5 Borehole Devices 4 Large Borehole Devices 3 Custom-Made Products

Appendix 10B: **Fields and Application of Hytec's Products**

Underwater

Fields	Applications
Oil and gas offshore operations (drilling well-heads, platforms, pipes) Energy and telecommunication cables Various submerged structures Oceanography Archaeology Marine geology Defence	TV systems for assistance to ultra-deep drilling operations Explosion-proof video monitoring systems for surface applications Assistance and control of remotely controlled sub-sea operations Assistance in laying and installation of pipes and cables on the sea bed Inspection and maintenance of sub-sea structures Assistance and surveillance of sub-sea works done by divers Search, localisation and recovery of submerged bodies Observation, inspection and counting of fauna and flora Oceanographic works Geological observation, measurement and sampling

Nuclear

Fields	Applications
Nuclear research centres Nuclear fuel production and conversion plants Nuclear power stations Nuclear waste stockpiling and processing centres	TV inspection and remote handling assistance for control of structures within : - reactor cores - tube sheets and steam generator pipes - pressurizers - fuel storage pools Assistance for remotely monitored and transmitted maintenance operations Assistance for automatic welding operations Assistance for decontamination operations Assistance for decommissioning operations

Pipe and Boreholes

Fields	Applications
TV inspection of the internal structure of pipes Inclination measurement Detection and measurement of deposits Measurement of cracks or corrosion pits by laser Pipe profiling and deformation/deflection measurement by scanning laser Detection and localisation of leaks Duct cleaning	TV inspection Measurement by laser Trajectory measurement TV inspection and work inside large bore piping in service Ducts profiling and measurement of sediments volume Cleaning of large ducts in service